THIS WEEK
AT CO-OP
presents...

A Collection of
Favourite Recipes
from the

D1457007

*Recipes developed and
collection compiled by:*
Linda Whitworth PHEc
Susan Spicer PHEc
Sylvia Kong PHEc

Copyright 1994 Calgary Co-operative Association Limited

Canadian Cataloguing in Publication Date

Whitworth, Linda, 1956-
  This week at Co-op presents-

Includes index.
ISBN 0-9696943-0-X (v. 1)
  1. Cookery, I. Spicer, Susan, 1956- II. Kong, Sylvia, 1963-
III. Calgary Co-operative Association. IV. Title.
TX714.W54 1994   641.5   C94-910886-3

Editing and Food Styling by :
Linda Whitworth PHEc
Susan Spicer PHEc
Sylvia Kong PHEc

Recipes developed and tested by :
Calgary Co-op's Consumer Counsellors

Design by:
Dory Rikkonen

Photography by:
Calgary Co-operative Advertising Photographers

Introduction

April 30, 1990 saw the launch of "This Week At CO-OP".

Over the 4 years that we have been featuring recipes in this flyer, we have received thousands of phone calls and letters requesting a cookbook. FINALLY!! we've compiled many of your favourite recipes from the first two years into this book. There are hundreds more that just wouldn't fit so we chose those that were the most requested. If this collection is well received, we have many more to include in the next volume. We continue to develop new recipes for "This Week at CO-OP" all the time.

All the recipes used in the production of "This Week At CO-OP", are tested at least twice in our test kitchen. We start with ideas, usually thought up behind the doors of our offices, or in the test kitchen, or while we're driving to and from work, or while were on holidays in some exotic place (grandma's back yard is exotic, right???). Then the ideas are researched to ensure customer acceptance and accuracy through books, phone calls or taste buds. Each then becomes an original recipe, unique to the Calgary Co-op collection.

We are all pleased to have contributed to the culinary experience of Calgarians. Our wish is that you will share this book with your friends and families afar.

Bon Appetite!

TABLE OF CONTENTS

INDEX OF PHOTOS

Banana Coffee Shake

Enjoy a tropical drink for coffee lovers.

2/3 cup	strong cold Co-op coffee	150 mL
1 1/4 cup	Alpha Milk-2%	300 mL
1	large banana	1
2 cups	Beatrice Vanilla Ice Cream	500 mL

In a blender, process coffee, milk and banana until smooth. Add ice cream and process until smooth. Optional: garnish with whipped cream.

Serve immediately.

Makes 4 servings.

Mocha Frosted Milk Shake

This beverage is almost like coffee and dessert in one.

2 1/2 cups	strong cold Co-op coffee	625 mL
1/4 cup	chocolate syrup	50 mL
2 cups	Beatrice Vanilla Ice Cream	500 mL

Place all ingredients in a blender and blend until smooth.

Optional: Garnish with whip cream.

Serve immediately.

Makes 4 servings.

Apple Lime Margarita

Keep the blender handy to make up more of this heat quenching thirst beating cooler.

2 cups	Sunrype Apple Juice	500 mL
1 cup	lime cordial	250 mL
3	drops green food colouring	3
2 cups	crushed ice	500 mL

In a pitcher combine apple juice, cordial and colouring. Whir, in batches, with crushed ice, in a blender or food processor.

Makes 6 servings.

Fuzzy White Navel

Cool smooth peaches. Mmmmm!

2 cups	McCain's Orange Juice	500 mL
4 cups	Beatrice Vanilla Ice Cream	1 L
1 cup	Co-op canned peach slices	250 mL
8	ice cubes	8

In a blender combine orange juice, ice cream, peaches and ice cubes. Blend until smooth.

Pour into glasses. Garnish with fresh mint or peach slices.

Makes 8 servings.

Dry Mai Tai

These refreshers can be made up by the glass at the "bar" or multiplied by the number of drinks needed and served in a carafe.

2/3	cup	Co-op Club Soda	150	mL
1/4	cup	McCain's Orange Juice	50	mL
1/4	cup	Co-op Lemon Juice	50	mL
1/4	cup	Co-op Pineapple Juice	50	mL
2	tbsp	grenadine	25	mL
2	tbsp	simple syrup *	25	mL
2	tbsp	frozen limeade concentrate	25	mL
1	cup	crushed ice	250	mL

In a blender, combine all the ingredients. Blend until smooth. Pour into tall glasses. Garnish with sliced orange. Serve immediately.

Makes 2 servings.

* SIMPLE SYRUP
In a saucepan combine 2 cups (500 mL) sugar and 1 cup (250 mL) boiling water. Bring to boil. Stir to dissolve sugar. Boil for 5 minutes. Makes 2 cups. Refrigerate for up to 6 months.

Pina Colada Perfecto

Caribbean fans just can't resist this island combo.

1/4	cup	cream of coconut	50	mL
1/2	cup	Co-op Pineapple Juice	125	mL
		crushed ice		
		Club soda		

In a blender, or with a small whisk blend together cream of coconut and pineapple juice. Pour over crushed ice and top with a splash of club soda.

Makes 1 serving.

Cham Pain-less Punch

Combined in punch bowl, topped with scoops of raspberry sherbet this "fluffy" punch is perfect for the bridal shower or luncheon.

4 cups	Co-op Pineapple Juice	1 L	
4 cups	white grape juice	1 L	
8 cups	Co-op Club Soda	2 L	
4 cups	raspberry sherbet	1 L	

In a large punch bowl combine juices. Just before serving add club soda and top with small scoops of the sherbet. The melting sherbet develops a lovely cream-like topping to the punch.

Makes 16 - 20 servings.

Sangria

A very satisfying drink on a hot evening!

1	orange	1
1/4 cup	sugar	50 mL
2 cups	McCain's Orange Juice	500 mL
1	bottle (26 oz/750 mL) dry red wine	750 mL
1/2 cup	orange flavoured liqueur	125 mL
	peeled sliced fresh fruit (oranges, lemons)	
	Co-op Club Soda	

Thinly peel off the outer coating of 1/2 the orange.

In a bowl, rub the sugar and peel together. This releases the oils in the skin.

Add the orange juice, red wine and liqueur. Cover for 15 minutes. Remove orange rind. Cover and chill for several hours so that the flavours will combine.

Serve in a punch bow garnished with sliced fresh fruit.

Add a touch of soda to each glass.

Sober Sangria - Another Refreshing Beverage

2 cups	Co-op Cranberry Juice, chilled	500 mL
3 cups	McCain's Orange Juice, chilled	750 mL
2 tbsp	Co-op Lemon Juice	25 mL
4 cups	raspberry soda, chilled	1 L

Combine juices and chill. At serving time, add chilled raspberry soda.

Yield 8 - 9 cups.

Coffee Liqueur

3 1/2 cups	sugar	875 mL
1 cup	water	250 mL
1	vanilla bean	1
1/4 cup	Co-op Instant Coffee	50 mL
1/4 cup	boiling water	50 mL
1	bottle (26 oz/750 mL) vodka	1
1 tbsp	Co-op Vanilla	15 mL
1 tsp	glycerine	5 mL

In a small saucepan combine sugar, water and vanilla bean. Bring to boil and boil 20 minutes. Remove from heat. In a measuring cup combine boiling water and coffee. Add to syrup mixture. Cool. Remove vanilla bean.

To cooled mixture add vodka and vanilla. For extra smoothness add glycerine. Bottle and age at least 1 month before serving.

Makes 6 cups (1.5 L).

Crabapple Liqueur

8 cups	crabapples	2 L
4 cups	sugar	1 L
1	bottle (26 oz/750 mL) vodka	1

Use whole crabapples, but wash, remove stems and blossom ends.

Place in a large clean glass jar. A gallon jar works best. Use enough crabapples to fill the jar. Pour sugar over crabapples. Add 1 bottle (750 mL) vodka. Screw on top. Place in a dark cool spot. Rotate jar every day for 28 days to dissolve sugar. Strain off liqueur and discard fruit. Bottle in dark coloured glass jars to preserve rich ruby colour.

Store in a cool place.

Makes 10 cups (2.5 L).

Curried Nuts and Bolts

Once you get started, you'll never stop!

1 cup	West Canola Oil	250 mL
4 tsp	Tone's Curry Powder	20 mL
3 tbsp	Worcestershire sauce	45 mL
1 tbsp	Tone's Garlic Powder	15 mL
1 1/2 tsp	Tone's Onion Salt	7 mL
1 1/2 tsp	Tone's Celery Salt	7 mL
4 cups	round oat cereal	1 L
4 cups	miniature shredded wheat	1 L
1	bag, Co-op Stick Pretzels	1
2 cups	Co-op Unsalted Peanuts	500 mL
1	box 'Bugles'	1

Heat oven to 250° F (120° C). Place oil and seasoning in a very large roaster. Add all remaining ingredients and stir well to coat evenly with seasoned oil. Bake for 1 1/2 hours. Stir every 1/2 hour.

Makes 18 - 20 cups (4.5 - 5 L).

See photo page 9

Meatballs with Yogourt Dip

A Middle Eastern style appetizer. Serve with pita crisps.

MEATBALLS

1 lb	lean ground lamb or beef	500	g
1	Country Morning Egg	1	
1/4 cup	bread crumbs	50	mL
1/4 cup	pine nuts, chopped	50	mL
1/4 cup	finely chopped green onion	50	mL
1/4 cup	Co-op Raisins	50	mL
1/4 cup	finely chopped onion	50	mL
1/4 tsp	salt	1	mL
1/2 tsp	Tone's Crushed Red Pepper Flakes	2	mL
1/2 tsp	Tone's Dried Mint Flakes	2	mL
1/2 tsp	Tone's Dried Coriander	2	mL
1/2 tsp	Tone's Allspice	2	mL
2	garlic cloves, minced	2	

YOGOURT DIP

1 cup	Yoplait Plain Yogourt	250	mL
2 tsp	dried coriander	10	mL

Preheat oven to 400° F (200° C). In a medium size bowl, combine all meatball ingredients. Mix well. With wet hands, shape mixture into 25 - 1 inch (2.5 cm) balls. Arrange on an ungreased pan. Bake for 15 - 20 minutes until well-browned.

DIPPING SAUCE

Combine yogourt and coriander. Cover and refrigerate. The dip has a fuller flavour when prepared a day in advance.

Serve hot meatballs with dipping sauce.

Makes 30 - 36 meatballs.

Sesame-Ginger Beef Strips

Serve as an appetizer, or part of an Oriental style meal.

1 lb	sirloin steak	500 g

MARINADE

1/2 cup	sherry cooking wine	125 mL
2 tbsp	Co-op Soya Sauce	25 mL
1 tbsp	minced ginger root	15 mL
1	garlic clove, minced	1
1/4 cup	Co-op Honey	50 mL
2 tbsp	toasted Tone's Sesame Seeds	25 mL
2	green onions, finely chopped	2
	Wooden skewers	

In a shallow casserole combine all ingredients for marinade. Cut steak into thin long strips, and add to marinade. Cover and refrigerate.

Soak skewers in water before threading with beef. This helps to prevent the skewers from burning.

Remove meat and reserve marinade.

Thread beef slices onto wooden skewer. Broil or barbeque for 3 minutes on each side, basting with marinade once.

Makes 30 strips.

Pork Satay Sticks

Soak wooden skewers in water for 1 hour before use.
This helps to reduce the skewers from burning.

1 1/2 lbs	pork	750 g
	Wooden skewers	
MARINADE		
1/4 cup	cooking wine	50 mL
1/4 cup	Co-op Soya Sauce	50 mL
2 tbsp	sugar	25 mL
1/4 cup	finely chopped green onion	50 mL
2 tbsp	grated ginger root	25 mL
2	cloves garlic, minced	2
1 tbsp	West Canola Oil	15 mL
SATAY SAUCE		
1/2 cup	chopped onion	125 mL
3	dried chilies	3
2	cloves garlic, minced	2
1/2 tsp	Tone's Ground Cumin	2 mL
1/2 tsp	Tone's Ground Coriander	2 mL
1/4 tsp	salt	1 mL
1	can (207 mL) coconut milk	1
1 cup	Co-op Crunchy Peanut Butter	250 mL

Slice pork into thin strips.

In a large bowl, combine marinade ingredients and add pork. Marinate for 1 hour in the refrigerator. Thread meat onto skewers. Cook on a greased grill over high heat for about four minutes per side.

Serve with satay sauce.

SATAY SAUCE

In a food processor, combine sauce ingredients. Whir for one minute. Heat mixture in a sauce pan over low heat. Note: peanut butter and coconut burn easily. Serve sauce with Pork Satay Sticks or any other grilled meats. Extra sauce can be refrigerated for one week.

Bitterballen

A savory warm appetizer, can be frozen and re-heated in oil if made in advance, or served cold if desired.

2 tbsp	Alpha butter	25 mL
1 tbsp	grated onion	15 mL
2 tbsp	Co-op Flour	25 mL
1 cup	Alpha Milk-2%	250 mL
1 tbsp	chopped fresh parsley	15 mL
1 tsp	salt	5 mL
1 tsp	Worcestershire sauce	5 mL
1/2 tsp	Tone's Curry Powder	2 mL
2 cups	cooked ground pork	500 mL
1 1/2 cups	shredded Edam cheese	375 mL
1 cup	fine bread crumbs	250 mL
2	Country Morning Eggs, beaten	2
2 tbsp	water	25 mL
	West Canola Oil for frying	

In a large saucepan melt butter and saute onion until transparent. Add flour, stir to blend. Gradually add milk, stirring constantly until thickened. Add parsley, salt, Worcestershire, curry, pork and cheese. Stir until cheese has melted, cook for 5 minutes stirring often.

Cool mixture for several hours in the refrigerator. Shape by the teaspoonful into balls. Roll in bread crumbs, dip into eggs beaten with water, and re-roll in crumbs. Place back in refrigerator for 1 hour, or until ready to fry. Deep fry at 375° F (190° C) for 2 - 3 minutes until golden brown.

Drain on paper towelling. Serve warm or chill in refrigerator.

Makes 36 - 40 balls.

See photo page 9

Steamed Meat
Dumplings (Siumai)

The wrappers are available in the Produce section.
These steamed meat dumplings double as a tasty party appetizer.

1	pkg (16 oz/454 g) wonton wrappers (approx. 3 1/4 X 3 1/4 inch)	1

FILLING

1 lb	ground pork	500	g
1/2 lb	raw shrimp, finely deveined, shelled and chopped	250	g
1	can (227 mL) water chestnuts, finely chopped	1	
1	can (10 oz/284 mL) bamboo shoots, finely chopped	1	
1 cup	finely chopped green onion	250	mL
1/2 cup	finely chopped celery	125	mL

SEASONING

1/2 tsp	salt	2	mL
1/2 tsp	Tone's Pepper	2	mL
1 tbsp	sugar	15	mL
2 tbsp	Co-op Soya Sauce	25	mL
1 tsp	sesame oil	5	mL
1/4 cup	cornstarch	50	mL

DIPPING SAUCE

1/4 cup	Co-op Soya Sauce	50	mL
1 tbsp	rice vinegar	15	mL
1/2 tsp	sesame oil	2	mL

In a large non-metallic bowl mix filling ingredients. In a small bowl, mix seasoning ingredients and combine with filling mixture. Chill mixture for 1/2 hour.

Place a tablespoon of filling in the centre of a wrapper. Gather up the sides, letting the wrapper pleat naturally and expose the top of the filling. Flatten the top of the filling slightly and give the middle a squeeze. Flatten the base of the dumpling and place on a lightly greased heat-proof plate or a bamboo steamer. Place plate/steamer on a rack over boiling water in a pot or wok. Cover. Bring the water to rolling boil then bring the heat down to medium - just enough to keep the steam going. If more water is necessary, add boiling water. Steam dumplings for 15 - 20 minutes. Serve with dipping sauce.

Makes - 80 dumplings.
* Once the wonton wrapper package is opened, the wrappers should be covered with a damp towel to prevent drying. Unused wrappers can be frozen, wrap and place in freezer bag for up to one month.

Crispy Shrimp Balls

These crispy treats will long be remembered!

1	lb	fresh shrimp	500	g
2	tbsp	lard	25	mL
4		water chestnuts, finely chopped	4	
1/4	cup	water	50	mL
2	tbsp	cornstarch	25	mL
2		Co-op Egg whites	2	
1	tsp	salt	5	mL
1/2	tsp	Tone's Black Pepper	2	mL
1	tbsp	sesame oil	15	mL
2	tbsp	finely chopped green onion	25	mL
2	tbsp	grated fresh ginger root	25	mL
1	tbsp	cooking wine	15	mL
10		slices, Co-op White Bread	10	
3	cups	West Canola Oil	750	mL

Shell, devein and wash shrimp. Pat dry. Place shrimp in food processor. Add lard. Whir until a smooth paste is formed. Add finely chopped water chestnuts.

In a small bowl combine cornstarch and water. Add cornstarch mixture to shrimp. Blend well. Transfer mixture to a large bowl. Gradually stir in egg white. Add salt, pepper, sesame oil, green onion, ginger and wine. Combine mixture and set aside.

In a wok or fryer heat oil to 375° F (190° C).

Remove crusts from bread. Cut bread into very small cubes. Place bread cubes on a large plate.

Shape shrimp mixture into 1 inch (2.5 cm) balls. Roll balls in bread mixture until evenly coated with bread cubes.

Deep fry balls 2 or 3 at a time. Cook 8 minutes or until lightly golden. Remove balls from oil and drain on paper towel.

Makes 24 - 30 shrimp balls.

Deep Fried
Mozzarella Fingers

These can be prepared in advance and then deep-fried just prior to serving.
They are a real delicacy when dipped in hot pepper jelly.

1 lb	Armstrong Mozzarella Cheese	450 g
1/2 cup	Co-op Flour	125 mL
3	Country Morning Eggs, beaten	3
1 cup	finely ground bread crumbs	250 mL
1/2 tsp	seasoned salt	2 mL
2 cups	West Canola Oil	500 mL

Cut mozzarella into 2 X 1/4 inch (5 X 1/2 cm) fingers. Roll the fingers in flour, then in egg, and then in bread crumbs. Roll a second time in egg and bread crumbs. Heat oil to 375° F (190° C) in a wok. Once oil is hot, fry a few mozzarella fingers at a time, until they reach a deep brown (approximately 30 seconds). Place on a paper towel and blot off excess oil. Serve while hot.

Makes 8 servings.

Cornmeal Parmesan Chicken Wings

These crispy crunchy wings are a hit at any get together.
They can be prepared in advance and deep-fried, just prior to serving.

2 lbs	chicken wings, separated	1 kg
1/2 cup	lime juice	125 mL
1/2 cup	Co-op Flour	125 mL
1/2 cup	cornmeal	125 mL
1/4 cup	Alpha Grated Parmesan Cheese	50 mL
1/2 tsp	salt	2 mL
1/4 tsp	Tone's Black Pepper	1 mL
1/4 tsp	Tone's Basil	1 mL
1/2 tsp	Tone's Oregano	2 mL
2	Country Morning Eggs, beaten	2
	West Canola Oil for deep-frying	

Marinate wings in lime juice for 1 hour. In a medium sized mixing bowl combine flour, cornmeal, parmesan cheese and spices.

After 1 hour remove wings from the lime juice and dip in the beaten egg. Next coat it in the flour mixture. In a wok or deep fryer heat oil to 375° F (190° C).

Deep fry wings for approximately 8 minutes. If the oil is too hot the wings will brown too quickly. If it is not hot enough the chicken will still be pink inside. Drain on paper towel.

Makes 4 servings.

Fiery Hot
Chicken Wings

These screaming hot chicken wings are easy to prepare, and can be made hot, hotter and scorching by adding more hot sauce. Enjoy these wings with celery sticks and commercial Blue Cheese Dressing to help extinguish any "fires".

2 lbs	chicken wings, separated	1 kg
3 - 5 tbsp	hot sauce	50 - 75 mL
2 tbsp	West Canola Oil	25 mL
1 tbsp	Co-op Vinegar	15 mL
1/4 tsp	Tone's Garlic Powder	1 mL

Set oven to "broil" and place rack 6 inches (15 cm) from the element. In a medium sized mixing bowl combine hot sauce, oil, vinegar and garlic powder. Place chicken wings on a broiling pan. Using a pastry brush, coat the wings with the sauce mixture. Broil the wings for 7 minutes on one side before turning them over and broiling for another 7 minutes.

You can also cook these wings over the BBQ. Cook wings for the same amount of time over medium high heat. Be sure to preheat the BBQ and brush the grill with oil to prevent sticking.

Makes 4 servings.

See photo page 26

Almond Chicken Wings with Plum Orange Sauce

The grated orange rind gives these wings a citrus flavour zing.

2 lbs	chicken wings, separated	1 kg
3/4 cup	Co-op Flour	175 mL
1	Country Morning Egg, slightly beaten	1
1 tbsp	Alpha Milk-2%	15 mL
3/4 cup	Co-op Ground Almonds	175 mL
1 cup	white bread crumbs	250 mL
2 tsp	salt	10 mL
2 tsp	grated orange rind	10 mL
	West Canola Oil for deep-frying	

PLUM ORANGE SAUCE

2/3 cup	Co-op Plum Sauce	150 mL
1/4 cup	McCain's Orange Juice	50 mL
1 tsp	cornstarch	5 mL

Toss wings in flour. Shake off excess.

In a bowl combine egg and milk. In another bowl combine almonds, bread crumbs, salt and orange rind. Dip chicken into egg mixture, then in almond mixture. Refrigerate coated chicken for 1/2 hour.

SAUCE

In a microwave safe bowl combine plum sauce, orange juice and cornstarch. Cook over high heat for one minute until sauce thickens and boils. Set aside.

Heat oil in frypan or wok to 375° F (190° C). Deep fry chicken for 10 - 15 minutes or until golden brown. Drain on paper towel. Serve with Plum-Orange sauce.

Makes 4 servings.

Pear Gruyere Quiche

The pear pieces are a fresh surprise in these bite-size pies.

3	Country Morning Eggs	3	
3/4 cup	Alpha Milk-2%	175	mL
1/4 cup	Alpha Whipping Cream	50	mL
1 cup	shredded Gruyere cheese	250	mL
1/4 tsp	Tone's Nutmeg	1	mL
1/4 tsp	Tone's Cinnamon	1	mL
1	pear (fresh or canned)	1	
24	mini tart shells	24	

Set tart shells on cookie sheet.

Cut pear into 48 pieces (if using fresh, peel pear). Place 2 pieces of pear in each tart shell.

In a medium bowl whisk together eggs, milk and cream. Stir in shredded gruyere, nutmeg and cinnamon. Spoon into tart shells.

Bake at 375° F (190° C) for 25 minutes or until golden.

Serve warm or at room temperature.

Makes 24 quiches.

See photo page 9

Cheesy Nacho Dip

A rich and spicy cheese dip for crisp corn or nacho chips.
A fun starter to a hearty BBQ or a meal in itself with a green salad.

1/3 cup	chopped onion	75 mL
2 tbsp	Alpha Butter	50 mL
1 lb	processed cheese, shredded	500 g
1/4 cup	Co-op Salsa Sauce	50 mL
1	can (14 oz/398 mL) Co-op Stewed Tomatoes	1
1	can (4 oz/114 mL) chopped green chilies	1
2	jalapeno peppers, finely chopped	2
1/4 tsp	Tone's Garlic Powder	1 mL
	Old Dutch Restaurante White Corn Chips	

In a skillet, saute onions in butter until transparent. Add cheese, salsa sauce, tomatoes, green chilies, jalapeno peppers and garlic powder. Stir, breaking up larger tomato pieces. Cover and cook over medium heat until cheese is melted. Remove cover, stir.

Serve with chips.

Makes 4 - 6 servings.

Lemon Vodka Prawns

A favourite starter or simple meal at fine restaurants.
The vodka is optional, but adds a zip to the dish.

1/4 cup	Alpha butter	50 mL
2	cloves garlic, crushed	2
1	lemon, juiced	1
1 lb	thawed or fresh peeled prawns	500 g
1/4 cup	sliced green onion	50 mL
2 oz	vodka	50 mL

In a large skillet melt butter and saute garlic until transparent. Add lemon juice, prawns and green onions and gently simmer until prawns are cooked through - about 3 minutes. Remove prawns with a slotted spoon and set aside.

Continue simmering sauce until it has reduced by half.

Add prawns and vodka and stir together just until hot.

Serve as an appetizer with toast points or a main course with steamed rice if desired.

Makes 4 appetizer servings or 2 main course.

Italian Tomato Bread

Fresh and spicy, prepare just before serving for best flavour.

4	medium tomatoes	4
1/4 cup	finely chopped onion	50 mL
1 tbsp	olive oil	15 mL
2	cloves garlic, minced	2
2 tsp	Tone's Basil	10 mL
1 tbsp	Alpha Grated Parmesan Cheese	15 mL
1	can (50 g) anchovy fillets (optional)	1
1/2 cup	sliced black olives (optional)	125 mL
	French or Italian bread loaf	

Wash tomatoes. Remove stem and coarsely chop tomatoes, skin on. In a mixing bowl toss tomatoes together with chopped onion, olive oil, garlic, basil and Parmesan. If desired chop anchovies, and/or olives and toss into tomato mixture. Slice bread through the middle of the loaf between the top and bottom crust. Cut into 2 inch (5 cm) slices. Just before serving, spoon fresh tomato mixture onto soft side of the bread slice and present open face.

Makes 4 - 6 appetizer servings (2 slices each).

See photo page 9

Mango Cheese Paté

A terrific make ahead appetizer; the flavours mellow if made a day or two in advance.

1		pkg (250 g) Co-op Cream Cheese	1	
1	cup	shredded Cheshire cheese	250	mL
1/2	tsp	Tone's Curry Powder	2	mL
1/2	cup	mango chutney	125	mL
2	tsp	brown sugar	10	mL
1		green onion, finely chopped	1	

In a small bowl combine cream cheese, Cheshire cheese and curry powder. Beat until smooth. On a serving plate shape into circle, 1/2 inch (1 cm) thick. Chill well. Combine chutney and brown sugar. Spread on top of cheese pate. Sprinkle with green onion. Serve on crackers.

Makes 6 servings.

Stuffed Prawns

Worth the effort!

12 - 16	large raw prawns	12 - 16
1/4 lb	lean ground beef	125 g
1	green onion, chopped fine	1
1/2 tsp	sesame oil	2 mL
2 tsp	Tone's Sesame Seeds	10 mL

BATTER

1 cup	cornstarch	250 mL
2	Country Morning Eggs	2
1/3 cup	water	75 mL
2 tbsp	Tone's Sesame Seeds	25 mL
	West Canola Oil for deep-frying	

Peel prawns leaving tail on. Butterfly by slicing through the back of the prawn. Do not cut all the way through. Remove vein and flatten slightly. Set aside.

In a small bowl combine ground beef, onion, sesame oil and sesame seeds. Divide and pat evenly over the cut side of each prawn.

In a blender or food processor combine cornstarch, eggs, water and sesame seeds. Pour into small bowl.

Dip stuffed prawns into batter. Deep fry in hot oil until cooked. Drain. Serve warm.

Makes 6 - 8 appetizer servings.

Cheesy Biscuits

To personalize your own biscuit add some grated onion, or chopped green pepper, some crumbled cooked bacon or even a handful of currants!

3 cups	Bisquick	750 mL
1/4 tsp	Tone's Cayenne Pepper	1 mL
2 1/2 cups	shredded Armstrong Aged or Medium Cheddar Cheese	675 mL
3/4 cup	Alpha Milk-2%	175 mL

In a large mixing bowl toss together biscuit mix, cayenne and 2 cups (500 mL) cheese. Add milk and stir to form a soft dough.

Turn out onto a floured surface and knead 6 to 8 times. Re-flour surface and roll out dough to a 1/2 inch (1 cm) thickness. Cut into 2 inch (5 cm) rounds with a floured cutter. Re-roll dough to use all of the mixture.

Top each round with a sprinkling of the remaining 1/2 cup (125 mL) shredded cheese.

Place rounds on an ungreased baking sheet and bake in a 450° F (230° C) oven for 15 minutes until biscuits are golden and puffed.

Makes 15 - 18 biscuits.

Rueben Lunch

A savoury package for the lunchbox, or warm straight from the oven.

3 cups	Bisquick	750 mL
3/4 cup	Alpha Milk-2%	175 mL
1 tbsp	hot mustard	15 mL
6	slices, Swiss cheese	6
1/2 lb	finely sliced corned beef	250 g
1 cup	sauerkraut	250 mL

In a mixing bowl combine biscuit mix and milk to make a dough. Turn out onto a lightly floured surface and knead 6 to 8 times.

Re-flour surface a roll dough out into a 12 X 18 inch (30 X 45 cm) rectangle. Cut into 6 even squares.

On each square spread a portion of hot mustard. Top with a slice of cheese, and an even portion of corned beef and sauerkraut.

To make packages, fold up four corners to a point on top and press together edges to seal and form a square "package".

Bake in a 450° F (230° C) oven for 15 minutes until dough is browned. Serve warm or chilled.

Makes 6 servings.

Cinnamon Wheels

The teabiscuit texture is delightfully sweetened with sugar and cinnamon.
Add raisins, chopped nuts or a little grated orange rind if desired.

2 cups	Bisquick	500 mL
2 tbsp	sugar	25 mL
1/2 cup	Alpha Milk-2%	125 mL
2 tbsp	Alpha Butter	25 mL
1/4 cup	brown sugar	50 mL
1/2 tsp	Tone's Cinnamon	2 mL
1/4 cup	Co-op Raisins	50 mL
2 tbsp	McCain's Orange Juice	25 mL
1/2 cup	icing sugar	125 mL

In a mixing bowl blend together mix and sugar. Make a well in the centre, pour in milk and mix with a fork about 25 strokes. Turn onto a lightly floured surface and knead 6 to 8 times. Reflour surface and roll out dough into a 8 X 12 inch (20 X 30 cm) rectangle. Spread with butter . Sprinkle with sugar, cinnamon and raisins. Roll up jelly roll fashion and cut into 1 inch (2.5 cm) slices. Place into greased muffin tin.

Bake in a 450° F (230° C) oven for 15 minutes until golden.

Remove from muffin tin. Cool slightly.

In a small bowl combine orange juice and icing sugar. Drizzle over cinnamon wheels.

Makes 12 wheels.

Miniature Cinnamon Orange Muffins

These delicate muffins are dipped in butter then cinnamon sugar.
An irresistible treat anytime.

1 1/2 cups	Co-op Flour	375 mL
1 1/2 tsp	Magic Baking Powder	7 mL
1/4 tsp	salt	1 mL
1/4 tsp	Tone's Nutmeg	1 mL
1/4 cup	Co-op Pecans	50 mL
1/3 cup	Alpha Butter	75 mL
1/2 cup	sugar	125 mL
1	Country Morning Egg	1
1/2 tsp	Co-op Vanilla	2 mL
1 tsp	grated orange rind	5 mL
1/2 cup	Alpha Milk-2%	125 mL

TOPPING

1/4 cup	melted Alpha Butter	50 mL
1/2 cup	sugar	125 mL
1 tsp	Tone's Cinnamon	5 mL

In a medium bowl mix flour, baking powder, salt, nutmeg and pecans.

In a large bowl with an electric mixer cream butter with sugar, then beat in egg, vanilla and orange rind until well combined. Add flour mixture to butter mixture alternately with milk, mixing after each addition just until combined.

Fill greased 1 3/4 inch (5 cm) muffin pans two-thirds full.

Bake in a 375° F (190° C) oven until muffins are golden brown, 18 - 20 minutes. Remove hot muffins from pans at once and dip quickly into the melted butter, then roll in combined cinnamon-sugar mixture to coat.

Serve warm.

Makes 18 muffins.

See photo page 41

Sunshine Muffins

A great start to the day!

2 1/4 cups	Co-op Flour	550 mL
2/3 cup	brown sugar	150 mL
1/2 cup	Co-op Unsweetened Coconut	125 mL
1/2 cup	Co-op Pecans	125 mL
1/2 cup	Co-op Raisins	125 mL
1 tbsp	Magic Baking Powder	15 mL
1 tsp	salt	5 mL
1 tsp	Tone's Cinnamon	5 mL
1 1/2 cups	grated carrot	375 mL
2/3 cup	Alpha Milk - 2%	150 mL
1/4 cup	West Canola Oil	50 mL
1 tsp	Co-op Vanilla	5 mL
1	County Morning Egg	1

In a large mixing bowl combine flour, brown sugar, coconut, pecans, raisins, baking powder, salt and cinnamon. Toss in grated carrot. In a small bowl or measuring cup mix together milk, oil, vanilla and egg. Add to dry ingredients. Stir only until dry ingredients are moist.

Spoon into 12 greased or lined muffin cups. Bake at 375° F (190° C) for 30 - 35 minutes until muffin springs back with lightly touched.

Makes 12 muffins.

Zucchini Seed Bread

*This moist, nutty, rough textured bread is so good
you will forget how healthy it is for you.*

1 1/2 cups	Co-op Flour	375 mL
1 cup	Co-op Whole Wheat Flour	250 mL
1/2 cup	Robin Hood Oat Bran	125 mL
1 tsp	Magic Baking Powder	5 mL
1 tsp	Co-op Baking Soda	5 mL
1 tsp	salt	5 mL
1/2 tsp	Tone's Cinnamon	2 mL
1/2 cup	sunflower seeds	125 mL
1/2 cup	Co-op Raisins	125 mL
3	Country Morning Eggs	3
1 1/2 cups	brown sugar	375 mL
1 cup	West Canola Oil	250 mL
2 tsp	Co-op Vanilla	10 mL
2 tsp	grated orange rind	10 mL
4 cups	finely shredded, unpeeled zucchini	1 L

In a large mixing bowl combine flours, oat bran, baking powder, soda, salt, cinnamon, sunflower seeds and raisins.

In a second bowl beat together eggs, sugar, oil and vanilla. Make a well in the dry ingredients, pour in egg mixture and stir until moistened. Stir in grated zucchini and orange rind just until mixed.

Tin Can Method: For our photograph we used 2 large (1 L) metal juice cans. Remove one end of the can. Grease and flour the interior. Fill each one with 1/2 of the batter. Place on a cookie tray to catch batter and place on bottom rack of a 350° F (180° C) oven. Bake for 1 1/2 - 2 hours until an inserted knife comes out clean.

Note: Batter will also fill 2 - 9 inch (2 L) well greased and floured loaf pans. Bake for 1 hour in a 350° F (180° C) oven until done.

Makes 2 loaves.

Simple Banana Bread

This is the straight goods, if desired 1 cup (250 mL) of nuts, raisins, chocolate chips or coconut, or 1 1/2 cups (375 mL) of any mixture of the above could be added.

3 cups	Bisquick	750 mL
1/2 cup	sugar	125 mL
1/2 tsp	Co-op Baking Soda	2 mL
2	large bananas, peeled and mashed	2
2	Country Morning Eggs	2
1/2 cup	Yoplait Plain Yogourt	125 mL

In a bowl blend together mix, sugar and soda. In another bowl beat together mashed banana, eggs and yogourt. Stir into dry ingredients and blend well. Pour into a greased 9 X 5 inch (2 L) loaf pan and bake in a 350° F (180° C) oven 1 hour until an inserted tester comes out clean.

For muffins bake 20 - 25 minutes in a greased muffin tin. Flavour and texture improve if wrapped and stored 12 hours before serving.

Makes 1 loaf or 12 muffins.

See photo page 41

Potato Dinner Rolls

These are a family favourite. A stew just isn't the same
without these delicious buns to accompany it.

1/2	cup	melted Alpha Butter	125	mL
1/2	cup	reserved potato water or water	125	mL
1	cup	Alpha Milk-2%	250	mL
1	cup	mashed potatoes	250	mL
1/2	cup	sugar	125	mL
1	tsp	salt	2	mL
2		Country Morning Eggs	2	
2	tbsp	Fleischmann's Quick Rising Yeast	25	mL
6 1/2	cups	Co-op Flour	1625	mL

Over medium heat melt butter. Add potato water and milk, heat just to luke warm, set aside.

Put mashed potatoes and potato water mixture in a large bowl. Add the sugar, salt and eggs. Beat with a wire whisk until smooth. Sprinkle yeast over all and beat again.

Add 2 cups (500 mL) flour, beat until smooth. Mix in 3 1/2 cups (875 mL) of flour with a wooden spoon. Gradually add the last cup (250 mL) of flour, working it in with your hands by pressing flour into dough and turning dough over, until you have a firm dough.

Cover and let rise in the same bowl for 40 minutes.

Punch dough down, place on floured surface. Sprinkle dough lightly with flour. Press dough out with fingers to a square 1 inch (2.5 cm) thick. Cut into 1 1/2 inch (4 cm) squares. If knife gets sticky when cutting just dust with flour.

Shape each square into a ball by pinching all four sides underneath to seal. Place buns almost touching in greased round or square cake pans.

Let rise covered for one hour or until doubled.

Bake in a preheated 400° F (200° C) oven for 15 - 20 minutes. For a soft crust brush tops with margarine or butter . Cool on racks.

Makes about 38 - 40 rolls.

Hot Cross Buns

Don't wait for Easter to enjoy these fruity buns!

1 tsp	sugar	5 mL
1/2 cup	warm water	125 mL
1 tbsp	Fleischmann's Traditional Yeast	15 mL
4 cups	Co-op Flour	1 L
1 1/2 tsp	Tone's Cinnamon	7 mL
1/4 tsp	Tone's Nutmeg	1 mL
1/4 tsp	Tone's Allspice	1 mL
2 tbsp	sugar	15 mL
1 tsp	salt	5 mL
1/2 cup	Alpha Butter, softened	125 mL
2	Country Morning Eggs	2
3/4 cup	Alpha Milk-2%	175 mL
1/2 cup	currants	125 mL
1/2 cup	Co-op Mixed Candied Fruit	125 mL
3/4 cup	Co-op Flour	175 mL

In a large mixing bowl combine sugar and warm water to dissolve sugar. Sprinkle yeast over top, let stand 10 minutes until yeast is frothy. Combine flour, cinnamon, nutmeg, allspice, sugar, salt, butter, eggs, milk, currants and fruit with mixer. Beat with mixer for 1 minute.

Remove dough to floured counter and knead with remaining flour as necessary for 3 - 4 minutes.

Place in a greased bowl. Grease top and cover with a damp cloth. Place in warm spot until doubled in bulk (1 1/2 hours).

Punch down dough. Cut into 18 pieces. Knead each piece into a ball. Place on greased cookie sheet. Snip a cross in the top of each bun. Place in a warm place and let rise until double (1 hour).

Bake at 375° F (190° C) for 20 minutes.

Cross with your favourite icing.

Makes 18 buns.

Pizza Crust

*This recipe makes two pizza crusts. If you wish to only use one crust,
the other crust can be frozen in its unbaked form for up to one month.*

1 tbsp	Fleischmann's Quick Rising Yeast	15 mL
1 cup	Co-op Flour	250 mL
1 cup	luke warm water	250 mL
2 tbsp	West Canola Oil	30 mL
1/2 tsp	salt	2 mL
1/2 tsp	sugar	2 mL
2 - 2 1/4 cup	Co-op Flour	500-550 mL

In a large bowl mix yeast and 1 cup of flour, then mix in water, oil, salt and sugar.
Add 2 to 2 1/4 cups of flour or enough to make a soft dough. Knead until smooth
and elastic. Place in a lightly greased bowl, turning dough to grease all over.
Cover with a tea towel and let rise in a warm place for 1 to 1 1/2 hours or until
dough doubles in size. Punch down and divide dough in half.

Preheat oven to 425° F (220° C). Grease pizza pans and roll out dough on lightly
floured surface into a 12 inch (30 cm) circle. Place on pan. Let rise for 10
minutes. Put on topping and bake according to recipe directions.

Option: For a crustier bottom, precook dough slightly (about 10 minutes or until
edges are lightly browned). Then put topping on and cook another
10 minutes until cheese is golden brown.

To Freeze Dough: Spread dough onto pans, cover with plastic wrap and freeze.
Once frozen, put in plastic freezer bag. Keeps well for one month. Thaw
in refrigerator.

Makes 2 pizza crusts.

Savoury Calzones

Serve these stuffed pizzas along side a salad or bowl of soup.

1	recipe for pizza crust, page 47	1	
1 cup	finely chopped parsley leaves	250	mL
2 tsp	Tone's Basil	10	mL
1/2 cup	Ricotta cheese	125	mL
1/2 cup	Alpha Grated Parmesan Cheese	125	mL
1 cup	shredded Armstrong Cheddar Cheese	250	mL
2 tbsp	olive oil	30	mL

Preheat oven to 425° F (220° C). Use pizza crust recipe and cut into eight portions. Shape into 7 inch (18 cm) ovals. Place dough ovals on a baking sheet, ready to be filled.

FILLING

Place all ingredients in blender or food processor and blend until mixture is a smooth paste consistency.

TO FILL DOUGH

Spread 1/8 of filling on half of pizza dough oval, leaving 1/2 inch (1 cm) border. Brush edges of dough with water. Fold other half of dough over top of filling to form a turnover, pressing edges together. Use a fork to seal edges decoratively. With the top of a knife, make three steam vents on top of turnover. Place in preheated oven and bake 15 minutes; lower heat to 350° F (180° C) and bake another 15 minutes.

Serve warm.

Makes 8 calzones.

See photo page 25

Meatball Pizza

A hearty pizza that will satisfy even the biggest appetite.

CRUST

1	premade 12 inch (30 cm) pizza shell or 1/2 pizza crust recipe	1

MEATBALLS

1/2	lb	ground beef	125 g
1/2	cup	bread crumbs	125 mL
1		County Morning Egg	1
1	tsp	Tone's Italian Herbs	5 mL
1/2	tsp	salt	2 mL
1/4	tsp	Tone's Pepper	1 mL

TOPPING

1/2	cup	pizza sauce	125 mL
1/2		green pepper, chopped	1/2
1/4	cup	chopped onions	50 mL
1	cup	shredded Armstrong Mozzarella Cheese	250 mL
Pinch		Tone's Crushed Red Pepper	Pinch

Preheat oven to 425° F (220° C). In a medium size bowl combine ground beef, bread crumbs, egg, herbs, salt and pepper. Form meat mixture into 1 inch (2.5 cm) balls. (Makes about 30 meatballs.) Place half of the meatballs in a microwave safe plate and cover loosely with wax paper to prevent splattering. Microwave on medium-high for 1 - 1 1/2 minutes. (Some of the meatballs will look pinkish in colour, but they will be further cooked in the oven.) Remove from plate, drain fat, then microwave remaining meatballs and set aside.

On pizza shell, spread pizza sauce. Sprinkle with peppers, onions and meatballs. Cover with cheese. Sprinkle with crushed red pepper. Bake 20 minutes.

Makes 1 - 12 inch (30 cm) pizza.

Wild Rice Soup

An elegant start to a meal of salmon, poultry or pork.
The nutty flavour of wild rice is perfectly highlighted with the herbs.

1 tbsp	Alpha Butter	15 mL
1	medium carrot, grated	1
1	medium zucchini, grated	1
1 cup	sliced mushrooms	250 mL
1/2 cup	onion, finely chopped	125 mL
4 cups	prepared Knorr Instant Beef Stock	1 L
1/4 tsp	Tone's Thyme	1 mL
Pinch	Tone's Pepper	Pinch
1	Tone's Bay Leaf	1
1/2 cup	wild rice, well washed	125 mL
1 tbsp	finely chopped fresh parsley	15 mL

In a large saucepan, melt butter and saute carrots, zucchini, mushrooms and onions for 5 minutes. Set aside. In a large saucepan, add stock, thyme, pepper, bay leaf and rice. Bring to a boil, reduce heat, cover and simmer 40 minutes. Add sauteed vegetables and simmer an additional 10 minutes. Add parsley just before serving.

Makes 6 servings.

See photo page 137

Strawberry Soup

This delicious creamy cold soup served with a croissant is ideal for a ladies luncheon.

2	cups	sliced strawberries	500 mL
1	tbsp	Co-op Lemon Juice	15 mL
1	cup	Beatrice Sour Cream	250 mL
1/2	cup	Alpha Creamo	125 mL
1/2	cup	Alpha Milk-homo	125 mL
1/4	cup	light brown sugar	50 mL
2	tbsp	orange flavoured liqueur (or McCain's Orange Juice)	25 mL
1	tsp	Co-op Vanilla	5 mL

In a food processor or blender whir together strawberries and lemon juice. Add remaining ingredients and process until smooth. Chill 1 hour.

Serves 6 servings.

Red Pepper Soup

A beautiful rosy colour soup full of robust pepper flavour.

2 tbsp	Alpha Butter	25 mL
1	large red onion, chopped	1
2	cloves garlic, minced	2
4	large red peppers, halved, peeled, seeded	4
4 cups	prepared Knorr Instant Chicken Stock	1 L
1 tsp	Co-op Lemon Juice	5 mL
1/4 tsp	Tone's Pepper	2 mL
	Salt to taste	
	Fresh or dried Tone's Basil	

In a large saucepan or Dutch Oven over medium heat melt butter. Add onion and garlic and saute until soft and fragrant.

Prepare peppers. Place skin side up on a baking sheet. Broil until skin is blackened and puffed. Remove from oven and place peppers in a plastic bag to steam. When cool enough to handle, peel skin off. Cut into chunks and add to onions and garlic. Cook 2 - 3 minutes. Add stock and simmer for 20 minutes. Add lemon juice.

In a blender or food processor whir mixture in batches until smooth. Season with pepper and salt. Serve hot garnished with chopped fresh or dried sweet basil.

Makes 4 - 6 servings.

Autumn Soup

Enjoy Autumn's bountiful harvest in this hearty fall medley. The use of a food processor will greatly reduce preparation time for this recipe.

1/4 cup	West Canola Oil	50 mL	
2	medium onions, chopped	2	
2	leeks, thinly sliced	2	
2	garlic cloves, minced	2	
4	celery stalks, chopped	4	
2	small turnips, peeled and chopped	2	
4	carrots, chopped	4	
2	medium parsnips, peeled and chopped	2	
1	red bell pepper, chopped	1	
1	green bell pepper, chopped	1	
2 cups	shredded cabbage	500 mL	
2	cans (14 oz/298 mL) Co-op Kidney Beans	2	
8 cups	water	1 L	
12	Knorr Chicken Bouillon Cubes	12	
1 tsp	Tone's Basil	5 mL	
1 pinch	Tone's Rosemary	2 mL	
1	Tone's Bay Leaf	1	
2 tbsp	Co-op Lemon Juice	25 mL	
1 tsp	salt	5 mL	
1 lb	spicy Italian sausage	500 g	
1 cup	fresh spinach, shredded	250 mL	
1/4 cup	fresh parsley, minced	50 mL	
1/4 tsp	Tone's Pepper	1 mL	

Heat oil in large sauce pan or Dutch Oven over medium heat. Add onions, leeks, and garlic and saute until onion is soft and translucent, about 8 minutes. Add celery, turnips, carrots, parsnips, bell peppers, cabbage and kidney beans. In a separate bowl or pitcher dissolve bouillon into water. Add this stock to the vegetable mixture. Add basil, rosemary, bay leaf, lemon juice, salt and pepper. Bring soup to a boil and simmer 30 minutes.

Fry sausages in a skillet over medium heat until they are brown all the way through. Drain on paper towels. Cut sausages into 1/2" (1 cm) thick slices. Once 30 minutes is finished add sausages, spinach and parsley and simmer a further 5 minutes.

Makes 10 - 12 servings.

Mad For Manhattan Chowder

Clams simmered in a spicy tomato broth with tender vegetables just can't be beat.

7		slices, Country Morning Bacon, chopped	7
1		medium onion, chopped	1
1	cup	chopped celery	250 mL
1/2	cup	chopped carrot	125 mL
1/2	cup	chopped green pepper	125 mL
1		leek white, sliced	1
2		cans (5 oz/142 mL) clams, reserve liquid	2
1		can (14 oz/398 mL) Co-op Tomatoes	1
1		can (10 oz/284 mL) Co-op Chicken Broth	1
2		potatoes, peeled and chopped	2
1/2	tsp	Tone's Thyme	2 mL
1/4	tsp	Tone's Pepper	2 mL
		Chopped parsley for garnish	

In a large saucepan or Dutch Oven saute bacon until just cooked. Drain fat to leave 1 tbsp (15 mL). Add onions, celery, carrot, green pepper and leek. Saute in bacon fat until onion is transparent, about 3 minutes. Add clams with liquid, tomatoes, broth, potatoes, thyme and pepper. Simmer for 20 minutes until potatoes are tender. Serve garnished with chopped parsley if desired.

Makes 6 servings.

Sunny Squash Soup

This pretty orange soup makes a lovely presentation
served inside the squash halves.

4 cups	cooked acorn squash (4 small whole squash)	1 L
1/2 cup	chopped onions	125 mL
1 tbsp	Alpha Butter	15 mL
2 cups	prepared Knorr Instant Chicken Stock	500 mL
1 tsp	grated orange rind	5 mL
1 tsp	Tone's Ground Ginger	5 mL
1 cup	Alpha Creamo	250 mL

Cut squash in half end to end. Place cut side down in a baking pan and bake in a 350° F (180° C) oven for 25 - 30 minutes until squash is cooked. Cool and then carefully hollow squash pulp from the skin leaving approximately 1/4 inch (1/2 cm) of squash around the shell. Set cleaned shells aside.

In a large heavy bottomed pot over medium high heat saute onions in butter until soft. Add squash pulp, chicken broth, orange rind and ginger.

Cover and simmer for 10 to 15 minutes.

In a blender or food processor puree squash-broth until smooth. Return to saucepan and slowly pour in cream stirring constantly.

Heat through, do not allow soup to boil. Serve in squash halves or soup bowls.

Makes 6 - 8 servings.

See photo page 57

Chow-Down Corn Chowder

Thick, gutsy chowders make wonderful comforting meals.

2	tbsp	Alpha Butter	25	mL
1	cup	cooked Country Morning Ham, diced	250	mL
1		medium onion, chopped	1	
2	tbsp	Co-op Flour	25	mL
1	cup	water	250	mL
1	cup	Alpha Creamo	250	mL
3	cups	Co-op Corn Kernels (fresh, frozen or canned)	750	mL
1		can (14 oz/398 mL) Co-op Red Kidney Beans, drained	1	
1	tsp	Tone's Curry Powder	5	mL
1/2	tsp	salt	2	mL

In a heavy bottomed Dutch Oven or large saucepan, melt butter over medium heat and saute ham and onions until onions are transparent. Stir in flour and cook 1 minute. Stir in water and continue stirring until mixture has thickened. Slowly stir in cream. Add corn, beans and seasoning. Continue to heat, but do not boil until corn has cooked, about 15 minutes.

Makes 4 - 6 servings.

Lobster Bisque

Ohhhh the calories, but ohhhh the flavour.

2	cups	frozen Lobster, drained, reserve liquor	500 mL
2	tbsp	Alpha Butter	25 mL
1/4	cup	brandy or cognac	50 mL
1/2	cup	chopped green onions, divided	125 mL
2		cloves garlic, minced	2
2	tbsp	Co-op Tomato Paste	25 mL
1	cup	white wine	250 mL
1	tbsp	Co-op Lemon Juice	15 mL
1/2	tsp	Tone's Thyme	2 mL
1/2	tsp	salt	2 mL
Pinch		Tone's White Pepper	Pinch
Pinch		Tone's Cayenne Pepper	Pinch
1		Tone's Bay Leaf	1
1/4	cup	Alpha Butter	50 mL
1/2	cup	finely chopped carrot	125 mL
1/2	cup	finely chopped celery	125 mL
1/4	cup	Co-op Flour	50 mL
3	cups	Alpha Milk-2%	750 mL
1	cup	Alpha Whipping Cream	250 mL
Pinch		Tone's Paprika	Pinch

In a large saucepan melt 2 tbsp (25 mL) butter. Add 1/4 cup (50 mL) chopped green onion and brandy. Bring to boil and simmer 5 minutes. Add reserved lobster liquor, garlic, tomato paste, white wine, lemon juice, thyme, salt, pepper, cayenne pepper and bay leaf. Simmer uncovered for 30 minutes. Strain. Reserve.

In a stock pot or other large saucepan melt remaining 1/4 cup (50 mL) butter and saute 1/2 cup (125 mL) lobster, remaining green onion, carrots and celery. Cook until tender, about 10 minutes. Sprinkle with flour stirring to combine. Add reserved liquid and continue cooking until thick and smooth. If mixture is too thick, add some milk. Puree mixture in blender or food processor. Return to saucepan. Gradually add milk and whipping cream, whisking until thick and creamy. Add remaining lobster and heat through.

Serve immediately garnishing with a pinch of paprika.

Makes 6 - 8 servings.

See photo page 105

Many Layer Salad

A great make ahead party salad with grilled meats. Just add rolls or garlic bread.

1/2	lb	fresh asparagus (or 1 pkg 10 oz/300 g frozen)	250	g
1/2	lb	fresh snow peas	250	g
1/2	cup	Italian salad dressing	125	mL
1		head butter lettuce	1	
1/2		purple onion thinly sliced	1/2	
1		head red leaf lettuce	1	
1		green pepper thinly sliced	1	
2	cups	shredded Armstrong Cheddar Cheese	500	mL
1	lb	Country Morning Bacon, cooked crisp, divided	500	g
1 1/2	cups	Best Foods Mayonnaise	375	mL
2	tbsp	Co-op Lemon Juice	25	mL
1	tsp	Tone's Curry Powder	5	mL

Clean and cut asparagus into 1 inch (2.5 cm) lengths and de-thread snow peas.

In a large saucepan bring 4 cups (1 L) water to a boil. Blanch asparagus and snow peas for 1 minute. Remove and immediately immerse in ice water to stop cooking. Drain. Toss asparagus and snow peas with Italian salad dressing. Set aside in refrigerator for 1 hour. Drain.

In a 9 X 13 inch (3 L) pyrex dish or large glass salad bowl layer butter lettuce, onion, red lettuce, asparagus and snow peas, cheese and 3/4 of the bacon.

In a small bowl combine mayonnaise, lemon juice and curry powder. Spread over the top of the salad. Refrigerate 24 hours. Sprinkle with remaining bacon.

Makes 8 servings.

See photo page 138

Japanese Cabbage Salad

The crunchy Japanese soup noodles and seasonings make the difference from everyday coleslaw.

SALAD

1/2 cup	Co-op Slivered Almonds, toasted	125 mL
2 tbsps	Tone's Sesame Seeds, toasted	25 mL
4 cups	shredded cabbage	1 L
2 cups	bean sprouts	500 mL
2 cups	sliced mushrooms	500 mL
4	green onions, sliced	4
1/4 cup	sunflower seeds (optional)	50 mL
2 cups	dry chow mein noodles	500 mL

DRESSING

1/2 cup	West Canola Oil	125 mL
2-4 tbsps	Co-op Soya Sauce	25-50 mL
1/4 cup	Co-op Vinegar	50 mL
1 tbsp	sugar	15 mL
1	pkg Co-op Instant Oriental Noodle Soup seasoning (any flavour)	1
	pepper to taste	

TOPPING

1	pkg Co-op Instant Oriental Soup Noodles	1

Toss together salad ingredients. Just before serving, add dressing to salad. Sprinkle salad with Instant oriental noodles.

Makes 8 servings.

Calico Salad

A mixture of some of Canadian's favourite vegetables marinated in a dill dressing. Best made the day before serving.

1	can (14 oz/398 mL) Co-op Kernel Corn	1
1	can (14 oz/398 mL) Co-op Red Kidney Beans	1
1	can (14 oz/398 mL) lima beans	1
1 cup	finely sliced carrot coins	250 mL
1/2 cup	sugar	125 mL
1/2 cup	red wine vinegar	125 mL
1/2 tsp	Tone's Dry Mustard	2 mL
1 tsp	Tone's Dill Weed	5 mL
1/4 tsp	Tone's Garlic Salt	1 mL

Drain liquid from cans. Combine corn, beans and carrots in a non-metallic bowl.

In a small saucepan stir together remaining ingredients. Heat and stir just until sugar is melted. Cool.

Toss vinegarette into vegetable mixture. Cover and marinate for 12 to 24 hours in the refrigerator. Serve chilled.

Makes 8 servings.

See photo page 122

Wild Rice and Apricot Salad

Canadian wild rice, mixed with brown rice provides interesting colour and texture to this refreshing cold pilaff.

4	cups	cooked wild and brown rice	1	L
1	cup	skinned, pitted and chopped apricots	250	mL
1/2	cup	finely sliced celery	125	mL
2		green onions, finely sliced	2	
1/4	cup	raspberry vinegar	50	mL
1	tsp	sugar	5	mL
2	tbsp	West Canola Oil	25	mL
1/2	tsp	salt	2	mL
1/2	tsp	Tone's Pepper	2	mL

In a salad bowl combine cooled cooked rice with apricots, celery and green onion.

In a small saucepan combine remaining ingredients and heat over medium temperature just until sugar is melted. Cool.

Toss into rice mixture. Chill.

Makes 8 servings.

See photo page 122

Asparagus Mimosa

Mimosa is a garnish so named because it resembles the yellow mimosa flower.

1 lb	asparagus	500 g
2	hard boiled Country Morning Eggs	2
1/4 cup	McCain's Orange Juice	50 mL
2 tsp	West Canola Oil	10 mL
1 tsp	wine vinegar	5 mL
1 tsp	grated orange rind	5 mL

Cook asparagus until tender. Drain. Arrange on plate and refrigerate.

Shell eggs and separate yolk from white. Finely chop yolks and whites separately. Set aside. In a small bowl, combine orange juice, oil and vinegar. Pour mixture over asparagus. Garnish with yolk, whites and orange rind. Serve chilled.

Makes 6 servings.

Patio Shell Salad

A light salad to accompany a Mexican style meal, or any grilled meats.

1/2 cup	Catelli Small Pasta Shells	125 mL
1	can (14 oz/398 mL) Co-op Red Kidney Beans, well drained	1
1	can (12 oz/341 mL) Co-op Corn, well drained	1
4	finely chopped green onions	4
1	can (4 oz/114 mL) green chilies, chopped	1
1/2 tsp	Tone's Ground Cumin	2 mL
1 tsp	Tone's Oregano	5 mL
1 tbsp	Co-op Lemon Juice	15 mL
1/2 cup	Best Foods Mayonaise	125 mL
1/2 tsp	salt	2 mL
1/4 tsp	Tone's Pepper	1 mL

In a saucepan of boiling water, cook pasta until al dente (just tender). Drain well, rinse with cold water.

Toss gently with all other ingredients. Refrigerate for 2 hours before serving.

Makes 6 - 8 servings.

See photo page 74

Ensalada Fruita

A colourful and refreshing side dish for a spicy meal.

1	small head, iceberg lettuce	1
3	oranges, peeled and sliced	3
2	apples, unpeeled but cored and sliced	2
2	bananas, peeled and sliced	2
1	can (14 oz/398 mL) Co-op Pineapple Rings	1
1	can (14 oz/398 mL) small cooked beet slices	1
1/2 cup	chopped Co-op Peanuts	125 mL

DRESSING

1/2 cup	McCain's Orange Juice	125 mL
1/4 cup	West Canola Oil	50 mL
1/4 cup	red wine vinegar	50 mL

Finely shred iceberg lettuce. Place in the bottom of a large salad bowl. Layer remaining fruit attractively on top. Garnish with beet slices and chopped peanuts. Serve with dressing on the side.

Makes 6 servings.

See photo page 58

Company Turkey Stew

This stew is fancy enough to serve to company.
Using cooked turkey helps reduce cooking time.

1	medium onion, chopped	1
4	slices, Country Morning Bacon chopped	4
2	cloves garlic, minced	2
3/4 lb	small whole mushrooms	375 g
1/4 cup	Co-op Flour	50 mL
1 cup	red wine	250 mL
2	cans (10 oz/284 mL) Co-op Beef Broth	2
1/2 tsp	Tone's Thyme	2 mL
1	Tone's Bay Leaf	1
1 tsp	Tone's Pepper	5 mL
2 cups	cooked turkey, cubed	500 mL
2 tbsp	fresh parsley, minced	25 mL

In a large heavy pot, cook onion, bacon, garlic and mushrooms for five minutes, stirring constantly. Stir in flour. Cook over medium heat for two minutes. Stir in wine, beef broth, thyme, bay leaf and pepper. Simmer for five minutes until thickened. Add turkey. Cover and simmer for 15 minutes. Stir in parsley just before serving. Serve over rice.

Makes 6 servings.

Goulash with Spaetzle

Spaetzle are small dumpling-like noodles that soak up this rich gravy beautifully.

6	slices, Country Morning Bacon, chopped	6
2 lb	round roast	1 kg
1 cup	onion	250 mL
2	cloves garlic, minced	2
1 tsp	Tone's Caraway Seed	5 mL
2 tsp	Tone's Paprika	10 mL
1 cup	Co-op Tomato Juice	250 mL
1	can (10 oz/284 mL) Co-op Beef Broth	1
1	red pepper	1
1	green pepper	1

SPAETZLE

1	County Morning Egg	1
1/3 cup	water	75 mL
1/2 tsp	salt	2 mL
3/4 cup	Co-op Flour	175 mL

In a Dutch Oven over medium heat cook bacon until browned but not crisp. Remove. Cut round roast into 1/2 inch (2 cm) cubes. Brown in batches in bacon drippings. Return bacon and browned meat with onions and garlic to pot. Cook, stirring occasionally until onions are browned. Add caraway, paprika, tomato juice and broth. Simmer, uncovered, for 1 hour.

Cut peppers into julienne strips. Add to goulash, cover and simmer 30 minutes.

SPAETZLE

In a medium bowl beat egg well. Add water and salt. Slowly add flour to egg mixture until smooth. Boil water in a large saucepan. Using the tip of a teaspoon drop spaetzle mixture into boiling water in about 1/2 teaspoon (2 mL) drops. With a slotted spoon remove spaetzle from water when it rises to the surface.

In bowls, serve goulash on top of the spaetzle.

Makes 4 - 6 servings.

Mexican Beef Stew

Mexican Chorizo sausages are sold fresh in the meat department.

1 tbsp	West Canola Oil	15 mL
1 lb	stewing beef, cut into 1 inch (3 cm) cubes	500 g
1	medium onion, chopped	1
1	garlic clove, minced	1
8	slices, Country Morning Bacon, chopped	8
1 lb	Mexican Chorizo sausages	500 g
2	cans (10 oz/284 ml) Co-op Beef Broth	2
4	large potatoes, cubed	4
4	carrots, chopped	4
Pinch	Tone's Ground Cloves	Pinch
1/2 tsp	Tone's Cinnamon	2 mL
1/4 cup	Co-op Ketchup	50 mL
1	Tone's Bay Leaf	1
1/4 cup	fresh parsley, finely chopped	50 mL
1	can (19 oz/540 g) chick peas, drained	1
	Hot cooked rice	

In a large heavy pot or Dutch Oven heat oil over medium high and brown beef. Transfer beef to a bowl. Add onion, garlic and bacon to pot and cook for three minutes. Reserve with browned beef. In the same pot, brown sausages , drain fat. Cool sausages and slice. Return beef mixture and sausage to pot. Add broth, potatoes, carrots, cloves, cinnamon, ketchup and bay leaf. Cover and bring to a boil, reduce heat and simmer for one hour. Add parsley and chick peas and simmer an additional 15 minutes. Serve with rice.

Makes 6 servings.

Oyster Stew

This recipe is from Canadian Pacific's inaugural transcontinental train trip.
It was served to John A. MacDonald's guests on that historic run.

1/2 cup	unsalted Alpha Butter	125 mL
1 cup	celery, very finely diced	250 mL
2	carrots, shredded	2
6-8	green onions, finely minced	6-8
1	leek, thinly sliced	1
1/4 cup	unsalted Alpha Butter	50 mL
1/2 cup	Co-op Flour	125 mL
2 cups	Alpha Milk-2%	500 mL
2 cups	Alpha Creamo	500 mL
1	can (142 g) clams, minced	1
2 cups	fresh, large oysters	500 mL
1/2 cup	white wine or dry sherry	125 mL
	Salt and pepper to taste	
	Tone's Paprika	

In a large sauce pan melt 1/2 cup (125 mL) butter, add vegetables, stir until vegetables are well coated with butter. Cover, simmer 20 minutes over very low heat, stirring once or twice.

To make white sauce: In a saucepan melt 1/4 cup (50 mL) butter. Stir in flour and combine well. Whisk in milk and cream, stirring constantly. When smooth and creamy, add vegetables.

In a medium saucepan bring to boil minced clams in their juice. Drain oysters and reserve (liquor). Add oysters to clams, then add wine or sherry. Cook over low heat for 10 minutes. DO NOT BOIL. When very hot pour into creamed vegetable mixture. Stir over low heat. DO NOT BOIL.

Salt and pepper to taste. Mix thoroughly and set aside.

To serve, place 2 tbsp (25 mL) oyster liquor in bottom of plate. Pour soup on top. Sprinkle with paprika.

Makes 6 servings.

Rosemary Lamb Stew

Gently simmered lamb is always tender and memorable.

3	lb	lamb shoulder, boned and cubed	1.5	kg
2	tbsp	olive oil	25	mL
1	cup	chopped onion	250	mL
1		Tone's Bay Leaf	1	
1/2	tsp	salt	2	mL
1/2	tsp	Tone's Thyme	2	mL
2		cloves garlic, minced	2	
1/2	tsp	Tone's Ground Sage	2	mL
1	tsp	Tone's Rosemary	5	mL
1	tbsp	Co-op Lemon Juice	15	mL
2	tbsp	red wine vinegar	25	mL
1	cup	water	250	mL
2	tbsp	Co-op Flour	25	mL
4		medium potatoes, cubed	4	
2		medium zucchini, sliced 1 inch (3 cm) thick	2	
3/4	lb	whole mushrooms	375	g

In a large Dutch Oven over medium heat brown cubed lamb in oil. Add onion, cook an additional 2 minutes. Add seasonings, lemon juice, vinegar and water. Cover and simmer for 1/2 hour.

In a small cup blend flour with a little water to make a paste. Stir into simmering stew.

Add cubed potatoes, simmer another 30 minutes. Add zucchini and mushrooms and simmer for another 30 minutes. Serve hot.

Makes 4 hearty servings.

Spicy Lamb Stew

A tantalizing combination simmered to perfection.

2 tbsp	West Canola Oil	25 mL
2 lbs	boneless lamb, shoulder cut into 1 inch (2.5 cm) cubes	1 kg
2 cups	chopped onion	500 mL
3	cloves garlic, minced	3
1 tbsp	grated fresh ginger root	15 mL
1 tbsp	Tone's Ground Cumin	15 mL
1 tbsp	Tone's Coriander	15 mL
1/3 cup	Co-op Flour	75 mL
2	cans (10 oz/284 mL) Co-op Chicken Broth	2
1	lime, juiced	1
1	can (28 oz/796 mL) Co-op Tomatoes	1
1 tsp	salt	5 mL
Pinch	Tone's Pepper	Pinch
1 lb	sweet potato, peeled and cubed	500 g
2 cups	chopped cauliflower	500 mL
1	pkg (300 g) frozen spinach, chopped	1
	Hot cooked rice or noodles	

In a large heavy pot or Dutch Oven heat oil on medium high and brown lamb in batches. Transfer browned meat to a bowl. Add onion, garlic, ginger root, cumin and coriander to pot. Cook for two minutes. Stir in flour and cook for three minutes. Gradually whisk in chicken broth. Cook on medium heat for five minutes, stirring until mixture is thickened. Stir in lime juice, tomatoes, salt, pepper and lamb, breaking up tomatoes. Cover pot and simmer for 1/2 hour. Add sweet potato and simmer an additional half hour. Add cauliflower and spinach and simmer for 1/2 hour. Serve with rice or noodles.

Makes 6 servings.

Rosemary Lamb Stew . . . . . pg 71

Hotter Than Medicine Hat Chili

No beans, just finely chopped round steak and a spicy sauce make this chili a close cousin to a true Tex-Mex version. Popular in Chili Cook-Off competitions.

4 lbs	round steak	2	kg
1/3 cup	lard	75	mL
2	Tone's Crushed Peppers	2	
2	cloves garlic, minced	2	
1/4 cup	Tone's Chili Powder	50	mL
1 tsp	salt	5	mL
2 tbsp	Tone's Oregano	25	mL
1 tbsp	Tone's Ground Cumin	15	mL
2	small fresh jalapeno peppers, finely chopped	2	
2	large tomatoes, cored, peeled and finely chopped	2	
1 cup	Co-op Tomato Juice	250	mL
2	cans (10 oz/284 mL) Co-op Beef Broth	2	

CONDIMENTS

1 cup	finely chopped onion	250	mL
1 cup	Beatrice Sour Cream	250	mL
1 cup	crumbled cooked Country Morning Bacon	250	mL
	Old Dutch Restaurante White Corn Chips		
	Chopped red, yellow and green bell pepper		

Finely cut steak into 1/2 inch (2 cm) cubes. Set aside.

In a large, heavy skillet over medium high heat, melt lard. Add crushed red peppers, garlic, chili powder salt, oregano and cumin. Cook for 2 to 3 minutes. Add steak cubes in batches to fat-spice mixture and brown. Reserve browned beef. When all the meat is browned, return to skillet. Stir in jalapeno peppers, tomatoes and beef broth. Simmer over medium heat for 2 to 3 hours, stirring occasionally, until meat is very tender and sauce has thickened.

Serve with condiments placed in bowls for self-serving.

Makes 4 - 6 servings.

Chicken Chili Verdi

A chili variation, wonderful accompanied with rice.

2 lb	Country Morning Chicken Breast Fillets,	1 kg
	cut into 1 inch (3 cm) cubes	
2 tbsp	West Canola Oil	25 mL
1 cup	chopped onion	250 mL
1 cup	sliced celery	250 mL
2	cloves garlic, minced	2
2	cans (4 oz/114 mL) peeled, chopped, green chilies	2
1	can (14 oz/398 mL) lima beans	1
1	can (14 oz/398 mL) pinto beans	1
1 cup	Co-op Medium Salsa	250 mL
4-6	drops, red pepper sauce	4-6
	Hot cooked rice	

In a large frypan or Dutch Oven, in batches, brown chicken breast cubes in oil. Once completely browned, return all chicken to pan with onion, celery and garlic. Continue cooking until onion is transparent. Add green chilies, beans, salsa and red pepper sauce. Simmer for 20 minutes stirring occasionally. Serve over rice.

Makes 4 - 6 servings.

Vegetarian Chili

This vegetable chili is so spicy, you won't miss the meat!

2	tbsp	West Canola Oil	25	mL
2	cups	chopped onion	500	mL
4		cloves garlic, minced	4	
2		large red pepper, chopped	2	
1		large yellow pepper, chopped	1	
2	cups	chopped carrot	500	mL
4		large tomatoes, chopped	4	
1		can (28 oz/796 mL) Co-op Tomatoes	1	
2	tbsp	Tone's Chili Powder	25	mL
1	tbsp	Tone's Ground Cumin	15	mL
1	tbsp	Tone's Basil	15	mL
1	tbsp	Tone's Oregano	15	mL
1	tsp	salt	5	mL
1/2	tsp	Tone's Pepper	2	mL
1		can (14 oz/398 mL) Co-op Kidney Beans, drained	1	
1		can (19 oz/540 mL) chick peas, drained	1	
1	cup	sliced green beans	250	mL
2	cups	shredded Armstrong Monterey Jack Cheese	500	mL

In a large heavy bottomed Dutch Oven, heat oil. Add onions and garlic and saute lightly. Add chopped red and yellow peppers and carrots. Saute until onions are transparent.

Stir in fresh and canned tomatoes. Add seasonings and let simmer 10 minutes.

Stir in kidney beans, chick peas and green beans. Cook for another 15 minutes.

Adjust seasonings to taste.

Garnish with grated cheese.

Makes 8 servings.

Egg and Sausage Bundles

One bite into these savoury bundles will reveal a delicious filling with a hint of sweetness from the mango chutney. Puff pastry is found in the freezer section.

1/2 lb	County Morning Pork Sausage	250 g
1	County Morning Egg	1
1/3 cup	sweet mango chutney	75 mL
2 tbsp	chopped onion	25 mL
1/2 tsp	salt	2 mL
Pinch	Tone's Pepper	Pinch
2 tbsp	Tone's Parsley	25 mL
4	hard boiled County Morning Eggs	4
1	pkg (450 g) Co-op Frozen Puff Pastry	1
1	County Morning Egg, slightly beaten	1

Preheat oven to 475° F (245° C). In a medium sized bowl, combine sausage, egg, chutney, onion, salt, pepper and parsley. Set aside.

Shell hardboiled eggs and cut into halves. Set aside. Divide pastry in half. On a floured surface, roll half of the pastry into a 12 inch (30 cm) square. Divide into four squares. Place a 1/4 cup (50 mL) portion of the sausage mixture on each pastry square. Place half an egg (round side up) on each portion of sausage mixture. Lightly brush outer edges of square with water, fold pastry over and firmly seal edges. Repeat procedure with remaining pastry, sausage and eggs. Place bundles on a baking tray. Glaze with beaten egg and bake for 15 - 20 minutes, until golden brown. Cool on a wine rack, then refrigerate. Serve cold.

Makes 8 bundles.

Salmon Supper Pie

A great family supper dish which can also be served to special guests.

2 tbsp	Alpha Butter	25 mL
2 tbsp	chopped onion	25 mL
1/4 cup	Co-op Flour	50 mL
1/2 tsp	salt	2 mL
1 tsp	Tone's Ground Cumin	5 mL
1 cup	Alpha Milk-2%	250 mL
2	cans (7 3/4 oz/224 mL) Co-op Salmon	2
1	can (10 oz/284 mL) Co-op Sliced Mushrooms, drained	1
2 tbsp	fresh parsley, chopped	25 mL
	Pastry for double crust pie	

In a saucepan over medium high heat, saute onion in butter until tender. Add flour, salt and cumin. Cook 2 minutes. Add milk and continue cooking, stirring constantly until thick and bubbly. Flake salmon into saucepan along with juices and well mashed bones. Add mushrooms and parsley. Stir to combine.

Roll out pastry for two crust pie. Place bottom crust in a 9 inch (20 cm) pie plate. Fill with salmon mixture and top with second crust, cut centre slightly to vent steam. Brush with a little milk if desired. Bake in a 400° F (200° C) oven for 30 to 40 minutes or until pastry is puffed and golden. Slice to serve.

Makes 6 servings.

Seafood Casserole

The flavours of different seafood mingle for a delicious company dish.

2	lbs	any combination, lobster, crab, shrimp, solid	1 kg
		whitefish (cod, haddock) or scallops	
1	cup	prepared Knorr Instant Chicken Stock	250 mL
1/3	cup	Alpha Butter	75 mL
1/3	cup	Co-op Flour	75 mL
1	cup	Alpha Milk-2%	250 mL
1	cup	sliced mushrooms	250 mL
1	cup	shredded Armstrong Cheddar Cheese, divided	250 mL
2	tbsp	chopped pimento	25 mL
1	tbsp	Co-op Lemon Juice	15 mL
Pinch		Tone's Cayenne Pepper	Pinch
		Hot cooked rice	

Poach seafood in 1 cup (250 mL) water for 8 - 10 minutes. Drain and reserve liquid. Combine liquid with chicken broth. In a large saucepan over medium heat melt butter. Saute mushrooms for 5 minutes and blend in flour. Gradually add broth mixture and milk stirring constantly until thickened. Stir in 1/2 cup (125 mL) cheese, pimento, lemon juice, cayenne and seafood.

Pour into a greased 2 L casserole. Top with remaining cheese.

Bake in a 375° F (190° C) oven for 15 - 20 minutes until mixture bubbles.

Serve with rice.

Makes 6 servings.

See photo page 105

Cheesy Rice Beef Pie

The rice and cheese crust makes a tasty and unique base to this simple family supper dish.

1	cup	Co-op White or Brown Rice	250 mL
3	cups	water	750 mL
1 1/2	cups	shredded Armstrong Cheddar Cheese, divided	375 mL
1		County Morning Egg	1
1	lb	lean ground beef	500 g
1/2	cup	chopped onion	125 mL
1	cup	sliced mushrooms	250 mL
1		clove garlic, crushed	1
1		pkg (10 oz/300 g) frozen spinach, thawed and drained	1
1		can (10 oz/284 mL) Co-op Cream of Mushroom Soup	1
1	tsp	Worcestershire sauce	5 mL
3		Country Morning eggs, beaten	3

In a heavy saucepan with a lid bring water to a boil. Add rice, reduce heat to low and cover. Cook rice until water is absorbed and rice is fluffy and tender, about 25 minutes. Stir in 1 cup (250 mL) cheese and egg. Press this mixture into a 10 inch (25 cm) deep dish pie plate to form a "crust" for the filling.

To prepare filling: Brown ground beef with onion, mushrooms and garlic. Stir in spinach, mushroom soup, Worcestershire and eggs. Pour mixture into rice crust. Top with remaining 1/2 cup (125 mL) cheese.

Bake pie in a 350° F (180° C) oven for 1 hour. Allow to stand for 5 minutes before serving.

Makes 6 servings.

Chicken Cannelloni

These pasta tubes filled with chicken and cheese are then covered with a zesty vegetable sauce. Mama Mia!

1	can (19 oz/540 mL) crushed Co-op Tomatoes	1
1	zucchini, grated	1
2	carrots, grated	2
1	clove garlic, crushed	1
1	can (5 1/2 oz/156 mL) Co-op Tomato Paste	1
1/2 cup	water	125 mL
1 tsp	Tone's Mixed Herbs	5 mL
1/2 tsp	Tone's Chili Powder	2 mL
1/2 tsp	Tone's Pepper	2 mL
1 tbsp	West Canola Oil	15 mL
1 lb	ground chicken	500 g
1	small onion, chopped	1
1/4 tsp	salt	1 mL
1/4 tsp	Tone's Pepper	1 mL
1/2 tsp	Tone's Mixed Herbs	2 mL
2 cups	shredded Armstrong Mozzarella Cheese, divided	500 mL
14	Catelli Express Oven Ready Cannelloni	14

In a large saucepan combine tomatoes, zucchini, carrots, garlic, tomato paste, water, mixed herbs, chili powder and pepper. Bring to boil and simmer for 30 minutes.

In a large skillet heat oil. Brown ground chicken and onion. Add salt, pepper and mixed herbs. Let cool. Stir in 1 cup (250 mL) shredded mozzarella.

Fill cannelloni shells with chicken mixture.

Pour 1 cup (250 mL) sauce in the base of an 8 X 11 inch (3 L) pan. Place filled cannelloni shells on top. Pour remaining sauce over top.

Bake at 350° F (180° C) for 45 minutes. Sprinkle remaining cheese on top and return to oven for 15 minutes.

Makes 6 - 8 servings.

Turkey Calabash

A microwave quick fix to use leftover poultry or pork.

1/2 cup	chopped onion	125 mL
1/2 cup	chopped green pepper	125 mL
1	clove garlic, minced	1
2 tbsp	Alpha Butter	25 mL
1/2 tsp	Tone's Paprika	2 mL
1/4 tsp	Tone's Thyme	1 mL
1 tbsp	Tone's Curry Powder	15 mL
1/2 tsp	salt	2 mL
1/4 cup	Co-op Raisins	50 mL
1 cup	chopped, peeled apple	250 mL
1	can (10 oz/284 mL) Co-op Cream of Mushroom Soup	1
1/4 cup	Alpha Milk-2%	50 mL
2 cups	cooked, cubed turkey meat	500 mL
2 tbsp	chopped Co-op Dry Roasted Peanuts	25 mL
2 tbsp	Co-op Shredded Coconut	25 mL
	Hot cooked rice	

In a small bowl combine onion, green pepper, garlic and butter. Microwave on High 2 minutes stirring once until vegetables are tender crisp. Add seasonings, raisins, apple, soup, milk and apple. Stir well.

Place turkey in a 8 cup (2 L) microwave safe casserole dish, top with vegetable and seasoning mixture. Cover and cook 6 or 7 minutes until heated through.

Garnish with peanuts and coconut. Serve with rice.

Makes 4 servings.

Spinach & Smoked Salmon Cheesecake

An elegant and unusual luncheon dish, or slice thinly and serve as a first course or appetizer.

CRUST

1 1/2 cups	bread crumbs	375 mL
1/4 cup	poppy seeds	50 mL
1 cup	shredded Armstrong Part Skim Mozzarella Cheese	250 mL
1/4 cup	light Alpha Butter, melted	50 mL

FILLING

1/2 cup	finely chopped onion	125 mL
2	cloves garlic, minced	2
2 tsp	light Alpha Butter	10 mL
2	pkgs (10 oz/300 g) frozen spinach, thawed	2
1 cup	finely chopped feta cheese	250 mL
1 cup	Beatrice Light Sour Cream	250 mL
3	Country Morning Eggs	3
6 oz	lox smoked salmon, chopped	170 g

In a mixing bowl combine crumbs, poppy seeds, cheese and butter. Press firmly into a 10 inch (25 cm) spring form pan. Set aside and prepare filling.

In a small skillet, or in a microwave oven, saute onions and garlic in butter until onions are transparent. Drain thawed spinach well. In a larger mixing bowl stir together spinach, feta, sour cream, eggs, smoked salmon and sauteed onions and garlic. Pour onto crust. Bake in a 350° F (180° C) oven for 1 1/4 hours until middle of cake is firm to the touch. Serve warm or chilled.

Makes 6 main course, 12 - 14 appetizer servings.

Chicken Enchilada Casserole

A Mexican style lasagna with layers of seasoned chicken between tortilla shells.

1		large onion, diced	1
2	tbsp	West Canola Oil	25 mL
1		can (4 oz/114 g) green chilies, chopped	1
1		can (10 oz/284 mL) Co-op Cream of Mushroom Soup	1
2	cups	shredded Armstrong Cheddar Cheese	500 mL
2	cups	shredded Armstrong Mozzarella Cheese	500 mL
1	cup	Co-op Salsa	250 mL
2	cups	cooked chicken, cut into bite size pieces	500 mL
6		large, tortillas - corn or flour	6

In a large skillet heat oil and saute onions. Add chilies, soup and half the grated cheese mixture (1/2 Cheddar and 1/2 Mozzarella). Cook slowly until the cheese melts.

Line a buttered 1 1/2 quart (1.5 L) casserole with 3 tortillas. Cover with 1/2 cup (125 mL) salsa sauce. Layer with 1/2 the chicken pieces. Pour on 1/2 the cheese sauce mixture.

Repeat layers as above. Top with remaining grated cheese.

Bake at 325° F (160° C) for 50 - 60 minutes. Let stand for 10 minutes before serving.

Makes 6 servings.

Tortiere

A traditional Christmas Eve dish in Quebec. Always a favorite for any winter evening entertaining. Excellent served with baked beans and a salad.

6		slices, County Morning Bacon, chopped	6	
1	lb	lean ground pork	500	g
1/2	lb	lean ground beef	250	g
1		small onion, finely chopped	1	
1/2	cup	boiling water	25	mL
1		clove garlic, minced	1	
1	tsp	salt	5	mL
1/4	tsp	Tone's Pepper	1	mL
1/4	tsp	Tone's Celery Salt	1	mL
1/4	tsp	Tone's Sage	1	mL
Pinch		Tone's Ground Cloves	Pinch	
1	cup	mashed potatoes	250	mL
		Pastry for double crust pie		
		Sunrype Apple Sauce		

In a frying pan cook bacon over medium heat until cooked but not crisp. Add pork, beef and onion; cook until pork is lightly browned. Add water and spices. Reduce heat to simmer; cover pan and cook 45 minutes. Combine meat with mashed potatoes; cool slightly.

Meanwhile, line a 9 inch (20 cm) pie plate with pastry. Fill with meat mixture. Place top crust. Seal and flute edges, slash several times to vent steam.

Bake in hot oven 450° F (230° C) for 10 - 12 minutes. Reduce heat to 350° F (180° C) and bake 30 minutes longer. Let stand 10 minutes before serving. Serve with apple sauce.

Makes 5 - 6 servings.

Chilies Rellenos

*Served in the casserole dish for easy preparation, cooking and serving.
Canned peppers are generally quite mild and sweet.*

4	cans (4 oz/114 mL) whole green chili peppers	4
1 cup	grated Swiss cheese	250 mL
3	County Morning Eggs	3
1/4 cup	Co-op Flour	50 mL
1 tsp	salt	5 mL

TOMATO SAUCE

1/4 cup	onions	50 mL
1	clove garlic, minced	1
1 tbsp	Alpha Butter	15 mL
1	can (14 oz/398 mL) Co-op Tomato Sauce	1
1 tsp	Tone's Oregano	5 mL
1 tsp	salt	5 mL

Split chilies in half lengthwise and remove seeds - stuff chilies with grated cheese and put back together as a whole chili. Canned chilies are very soft, handle carefully. Arrange in one layer into a 9 X 13 inch (3 L) baking dish.

Separate eggs. Beat whites seperately until stiff. In another bowl beat yolks. Beat in flour and salt. Continue to beat until thick and creamy. Fold in egg whites. Spread mixture over chilies.

TOMATO SAUCE

Saute onions and garlic in butter. Add tomato sauce and oregano. Pour sauce over chilies and eggs.

Bake in a 375° F (190° C) oven for 30 minutes.

Serve with Mexican rice and refried beans. Serve hot.

Makes 4 - 6 servings.

Paella

This Spanish specialty derives its name from the pan from which it is served. The seafood can be varied according to your own tastes and availability.

1	lb	fresh mussels	500	g
2	tbsp	olive oil	25	mL
1	lb	boneless, skinned County Morning Chicken Breasts	500	g
1		can (5 oz /142 mL) steamed clams, reserve liquor	1	
1/2	lb	hot Italian sausage	250	g
4		cloves garlic, minced	4	
1	cup	chopped onion	250	mL
1 1/2	cups	uncooked Co-op rice	375	mL
1	cup	reserved clam liquor	250	mL
2	cups	water	500	mL
1	cup	coarsely chopped tomatoes	250	mL
1		can (14 oz /398 mL) Co-op Tomatoes	1	
1		green pepper, cut in strips	1	
1		red pepper, cut into strips	1	
1		Tone's Bay Leaf	1	
1		Knorr Chicken Bouillon cube	1	
1/4	tsp	saffron	1	mL
2	tsp	Tone's Paprika	10	mL
1/4	tsp	Tone's Tumeric	1	mL
1/4	tsp	Tone's Pepper	1	mL
1/2	tsp	Tone's Crushed Chili Peppers	2	mL
1	lb	cleaned raw shrimp	500	g
1		can (14 oz /398 mL) artichoke hearts, drained and cut into quarters	1	
1	cup	Co-op Frozen Peas	250	mL

Scrub mussels under cold running water. Cut off any hairy beards from mussels. Discard any mussels that do not close when tapped. Refrigerate mussels until required.

Cube chicken breasts. In a large Dutch Oven over medium high heat oil. Brown chicken on all sides until brown. Remove chicken and set aside.

Cut sausage into 1 inch (2.5 cm) pieces and brown in pan. Add onions and garlic. Stir in rice. Add clam liquor, water, chopped and canned tomatoes, green and red pepper, bay leaf, bouillon cube, saffron, paprika, tumeric, pepper and crushed chilies. Add chicken. Bring mixture to a boil. Reduce heat. Cover and simmer for 20 minutes.

Stir in shrimp and cleaned mussels, artichoke hearts, peas and clams. Cover and cook until piping hot (about 10 minutes). Discard any mussels that do not open.

Makes 8 servings.

Spicy Thai Noodles . . . . . . pg 91

Spicy Thai Noodles

The noodles are found in the Chinese section of the store.
Lime adds an interesting tang to this dish.

SAUCE

2 tbsp	West Canola Oil	25	mL
1/2 cup	sherry	125	mL
1/2 cup	Co-op Soya Sauce	125	mL
1/4 cup	Co-op Tomato Paste	50	mL
2 tsp	grated lime rind	10	mL
1/4 cup	lime juice	50	mL
1/4 cup	brown sugar	50	mL
2 tsp	Chinese chili paste	10	mL

VEGETABLES

1	pkg (454 g) dry Chinese style noodles	1	
2 tbsp	West Canola Oil, divided	25	mL
1 lb	pork thinly sliced	500	g
1/2 cup	sliced carrot	125	mL
1	red pepper, chopped	1	
1	pkg (454 g/16 oz) mixed chop suey vegetables	1	
1/2 cup	chopped fresh cilantro	125	mL
1	pkg (200 g) frozen raw shrimp	1	
1/4 cup	unsalted Co-op Dry Roasted Peanuts	50	mL

In a small saucepan combine all sauce ingredients. Bring to boil and cook until slightly thickened. Set aside.

In a large Dutch Oven bring 3 quarts (3 L) water to boil, cook noodles 5 minutes until just tender. Drain toss with 1 tbsp (25 mL) oil. Set aside.

In a wok heat 1 tsp (5 mL) oil. Quickly stir fry pork. Remove to a plate.

Add the remaining 2 tsp (10 mL) oil to the wok and stir fry the carrot, red pepper and mixed vegetables for 5 minutes. Add cilantro and shrimp. Cook until shrimp turns pink, about 2 minutes. Return pork to wok.

Add noodles and sauce. Toss together and heat through. Garnish with peanuts.

Makes 8 servings.

Corny Pie

Something different for ground beef.
Try ground chicken or turkey for a real change of pace.

1 lb	ground beef	500 g
1 cup	chopped onion	250 mL
1	clove garlic, minced	1
1 tsp	Tone's Chili Powder	5 mL
Pinch	Tone's Pepper	Pinch
1	can (14 oz/398 mL) Co-op Corn, drained	1
1	jar (10 oz/284 mL) Co-op Salsa	1
1	can (4 oz/114 mL) chopped green chilies	1
1	pkg refrigerator flaky biscuits	1
1/2 cup	shredded Armstrong Cheddar Cheese	125 mL

In a large frying pan brown ground beef, onion and garlic. Drain. Add chili powder, pepper, corn, salsa and green chilies.

Grease a 9 inch (22 cm) pie plate. Arrange biscuits evenly around the edge of the pie plate. Ladle beef mixture into centre of pie plate. Sprinkle cheese on top. Place in 375° F (190° C) oven for 25 minutes.

Makes 6 servings.

German Pork Bake

A comforting autumn supper, slow simmered to tenderness.

4	slices, County Morning Bacon, chopped	4
1 cup	chopped onion	250 mL
1	clove garlic, minced	1
4 cups	shredded cabbage	1 L
1	can (28 oz /768 mL) Co-op Tomatoes	1
1	jar (32 oz /909 mL) wine sauerkraut	1
1/4 cup	Sunrype Apple Juice	50 mL
3/4 lb	garlic sausage	375 g
2 lb	pork spare ribs	1 kg
1	green apple, chopped	1

In a large heavy bottomed Dutch Oven over medium high heat, cook bacon until crisp. Add onions and garlic. Cook until onions transparent. Add cabbage. When tender, add tomatoes.

Place sauerkraut in colander and rinse under cold running water. Drain and add to cabbage mixture with apple juice.

Cut garlic sausage into 1 inch (3 cm) pieces and ribs into riblets. Add to cabbage mixture. Stir in chopped apple. Cover and let simmer 2 hours until meat is tender.

Serve with boiled potatoes.

Makes 4 servings.

$1.49 Day Master Mix

This recipe is the key ingredient for the following dishes.
It is also very good on it's own (try it on a bun as a "Sloppy Joe"), or in any of
your other recipes which call for a basic meat sauce.

4 cups	chopped onion	1	L
2 cups	chopped celery	500	mL
3	cloves garlic, minced	3	
2 tbsp	West Canola Oil	25	mL
4 lb	ground beef	2	kg
3	cans (28 oz/796 mL) Co-op Tomatoes	3	
2	cans (5 1/2 oz/156 mL) Co-op Tomato Paste	2	
2	cans (10 oz/284 mL) Co-op Mushrooms	2	
1 tsp	Tone's Basil	5	mL
2 tsp	Tone's Oregano	10	mL
2 tsp	salt	10	mL
2 tbsp	Tone's Parsley	25	mL
1 tsp	Tone's Pepper	5	mL
1/2 tsp	Tone's Crushed Red Pepper	2	mL

In a very large Dutch Oven saute onion, celery and garlic in oil. Add ground beef, brown. Drain off fat. Add remaining ingredients and simmer 1 1/2 hours.

Divide into 4 batches (2 cups/500 mL each) and freeze. Or make into one of the following supper dishes and freeze.

Makes 8 cups (2 L).

"Everything but the Sink" Soup

Add whatever you want to this versatile recipe. Sinks not recommended!

2 cups	Master Mix (pg. 94)	500 L
2	large potatoes, cut in cubes	2
2	cans (10 oz/284 mL) Co-op Consomme	2
2 1/2 cups	water	625 mL
1 cup	grated carrot	250 mL
1/4 cup	Co-op Barley (pearl or pot)	50 mL
1 cup	chopped celery	250 mL

Place master mix in a large saucepan or Dutch Oven. Add remaining ingredients. Bring to a boil. Reduce heat and simmer 1 1/2 hours until barley is tender.

Eat immediately or freeze.

Makes 6 - 8 servings.

Spaghetti Special

With the Master Mix this sauce can be quickly put together, and has that simmered all day flavour.

2 cups	Master Mix (pg. 94)	500 mL
1	can (10 oz/284 mL) Co-op Sliced Mushrooms, drained	1
1	can (5 1/2 oz/156 mL) tomato paste	1
1 tsp	Tone's Italian Seasoning	5 mL
	Catelli Spaghetti	

In a large saucepan combine all of the above and simmer, covered for 1/2 hour. Serve over cooked pasta.

Makes 4 - 6 servings.

Shepherd's Pie

An old favourite, this savoury supper is fast and delicious with the premade Master Mix.

2 cups	Master Mix (pg. 94)	500 mL
3 cups	mashed potatoes, divided	750 mL
1	can (10 oz/284 mL) Co-op Mushrooms, drained	1
1 tbsp	Knorr Instant Beef Stock Mix	15 mL
1 cup	grated carrot	250 mL
2 tbsp	Grated Alpha Parmesan Cheese	25 mL

In a saucepan combine Master Mix, 1 cup (250 mL) mashed potatoes, mushrooms and soup base. Pour into 6 cup (1 1/2 L) casserole. With a piping bag and fancy tip decorate the top with remaining mashed potatoes. If desired, spoon the potatoes around the edge.

Sprinkle Parmesan cheese on top of potatoes.

Bake at 350° F (180° C) for 40 minutes or freeze and bake later.

Makes 4 servings.

Lasagna

A classic, rich, cheesy and saucy dish.

2	cups	Master Mix (pg. 94)	500	mL
1		can (5 1/2 oz/156 mL) Co-op Tomato Paste	1	
1/2	tsp	Tone's Basil	2	mL
2	cups	Beatrice Cottage Cheese	500	mL
1		Country Morning Egg	1	
6-9		Catelli Lasagna Noodles	6-9	
1	lb	shredded Armstrong Mozzarella Cheese	500	g
1/2	cup	Alpha Grated Parmesan Cheese	125	mL

In a small saucepan combine Master Mix, tomato paste and basil. Bring to a boil, reduce heat and simmer 30 minutes.

In a Dutch Oven boil 8 cups (2 L) water, cook lasagna noodles until tender.

In a small bowl combine cottage cheese and egg.

Pour 1/4 cup (50 mL) meat mixture into the bottom of 9 X 13 inch (3 L) baking pan. Place a layer of noodles, 1/2 of the meat mixture, 1/2 of the cottage cheese mixture, 1/2 of the mozzarella. Repeat with noodles, remaining meat, cottage cheese and mozzarella cheese.

Sprinkle with Parmesan.

Bake at 375° F (190° C) 40 - 45 minutes or freeze for later.

Makes 6 - 8 servings.

Herb Marinated Pork Chops

A plastic food storage bag is a handy container to marinate the chops.

1/4 cup	Co-op Lemon Juice	50 mL
2 tbsp	West Canola Oil	25 mL
2 tsp	Tone's Oregano	10 mL
2 tsp	Tone's Rosemary	10 mL
1/4 tsp	Tone's Pepper	1 mL
1	clove garlic, minced	1
6	pork chops	6

Combine juice, oil, oregano, rosemary, pepper and garlic. Place chops in a shallow non-metallic container and pour in marinade. Cover and marinate for one hour in the refrigerator. Remove chops and reserve marinade. Cook chops on a greased grill over medium high heat for fifteen minutes. Turn once and brush with marinade.

Makes 6 servings.

See photo page 106

Marinated Minted Lamb

A hint of mint and the subtle sweetness of this marinade are perfect for the flavour of roasted lamb.

5 - 6	lbs	leg of lamb	2 - 2.5	kg
1	cup	red currant jelly	250	mL
2	tbsp	red wine vinegar	25	mL
1	tsp	Tone's Dried Mint or	5	mL
		(1 tbsp - 15 mL) fresh chopped mint		
2	tbsp	olive oil	25	mL
2		cloves garlic, crushed	2	

Debone leg of lamb and butterfly. Ask your butcher to do this for you if possible.

In a small saucepan, combine red currant jelly and vinegar. Warm over low heat until melted. Remove from heat and stir in mint, olive oil and garlic.

Place lamb in plastic bag or non-metallic dish to marinate. Pour sauce over. Cover or seal and refrigerate 8 hours or overnight before barbecuing.

TO BARBECUE

A propane or gas dual burning barbecue is required for this method. Place a drip pan under the grill on one side of the BBQ. Turn the opposite burner on to HIGH. Place the lamb leg over the drip pan and leave this burner unlit. Close lid. The heat from the one side will cause a convection current which will "roast" the lamb. Baste often with remaining marinade except for the last 15 minutes of cooking. The roast does not require turning. Cook 20 minutes per pound (40 minutes per kg) for medium rare. Let stand for 10 minutes before carving.

Makes 8 servings.

Sweet and Sour Pork Ribs

Try this tangy oven recipe for ribs.

1 cup	chopped onion	250 mL
1 cup	chopped green pepper	250 mL
1 cup	E.D. Smith Triple Fruit Apricot	250 mL
1 cup	Co-op Ketchup	250 mL
1/2 cup	water	125 mL
1	can (14 oz/398 mL) Co-op Pineapple Chunks	1
1/4 cup	Co-op Vinegar	50 mL
2 tsp	Tone's Ground Ginger	10 mL
5 lb	pork side ribs	2 kg

In a large bowl, combine onion, pepper, jam, ketchup, water, pineapple, vinegar and ginger. Stir until well combined.

Cut rib into 3 inch (8 cm) pieces. Place in roasting pan dish. Pour sauce over top. Bake in 350° F (180° C) oven for 2 1/2 hours or until ribs are fork tender. Serve over rice.

Makes 4 - 6 servings.

Hoisin Ribs

The aroma of these ribs will make your appetite soar.

4	lb	pork spareribs	2	kg
2	tbsp	grated fresh ginger	25	mL
2		garlic cloves, minced	2	
1/2	cup	Co-op Soya Sauce	125	mL
1/2	cup	Hoisin sauce	125	mL
1/2	cup	Co-op Honey	125	mL
1/2	cup	dry sherry	125	mL
1/4	tsp	sesame oil	1	mL

Cut ribs into portions of two or three ribs. Set aside.

In a bowl combine ginger, garlic, soy sauce, Hoisin sauce, honey, sherry and sesame oil. Arrange ribs in a large baking dish and pour sauce mixture over top. Cover dish and marinate over night in the refrigerator.

Heat grill to medium. Cook ribs for twenty minutes on a greased grill, turning and brushing ribs occasionally with extra marinade.

Makes 6 servings.

Big Bucks Bill Junior's Beef Ribs

Cook the ribs slowly over low heat and baste liberally to produce a succulent Sante Fe style rib.

SAUCE

1 cup	Co-op Tomato Juice	250 mL
1/2 cup	Co-op Ketchup	125 mL
*1/4 cup	Extra Hot Chili Sauce *	50 mL
2 tbsp	Worcestershire sauce	25 mL
1 tbsp	Tone's Dry Mustard	15 mL
1 cup	finely chopped onion	250 mL
1/4 cup	Co-op Vinegar	50 mL
1 tbsp	Tone's Chili Powder	15 mL
2 tbsp	Co-op Molasses	25 mL
1/4 cup	brown sugar	50 mL
1 tsp	salt	5 mL
2	cloves garlic, minced	2
1/4 tsp	Tone's Pepper	1 mL
4-6	beef rib bones	4-6

In a medium sauce pan, combine all sauce ingredients. Place over medium heat and simmer 1 hour until thickened.

Preheat barbecue to medium high. Place ribs on barbecue and turn often to prevent burning. Cook 15 - 20 minutes.

Apply liberal coating of barbecue sauce to ribs. Move ribs to one side of barbecue and turn off burner on that side. Cook indirectly for an additional 10 minutes, baste occasionally to build a thick coat of sauce on ribs. Serve.

* For extra spicy flavour, add the hot sauce. To reduce the zing, omit.

Makes 4 servings.

Western Short Ribs

The result is a tomato BBQ flavour without having to watch the coals. Serve with rice and a tossed salad. Steamed broccoli is a good vegetable accompaniment if desired.

3 lbs	beef short ribs	1.5 kg
1	can (14 oz/396 mL) Co-op Tomato Sauce	1
1/2 cup	Co-op Molasses	125 mL
2 tbsp	Co-op Prepared Mustard	25 mL
1	onion, chopped	1
Few	drops, hot pepper sauce	Few

In a deep Dutch Oven or roaster, place short ribs. In a small bowl combine remaining ingredients and pour over ribs, coat well.

Cover and bake in a 350° F (180° C) oven for 3 hours until ribs are fork tender.

Makes 4-5 servings.

Indonesian Beef

Here's an easy way to enjoy a less expensive cut of beef! Plan ahead to marinate for 48 hours to tenderize.

3 lbs	beef short ribs (boneless)	1.5 kg
1/4 cup	West Canola Oil	50 mL
1/2 cup	Co-op Soya Sauce	125 mL
1/4 cup	brown sugar	50 mL
4	cloves garlic, minced	4
2 tbsp	Tone's Curry Powder	25 mL
1/4 cup	lime juice	50 mL
2 tbsp	grated onion	25 mL

Place ribs in a plastic bag or in a non-metallic container with a tight fitting lid.

In a small bowl combine oil, soy sauce, sugar, garlic, curry powder, lime juice and onion. Pour over ribs. Cover tightly (or seal bag). Place in refrigerator and allow to marinate 48 hours. Turn occasionally.

To cook, preheat barbecue to medium. Remove meat from dish, discard marinade. Place ribs on grill and turn often. Cook until well browned, about 10 minutes.

Makes 6 servings.

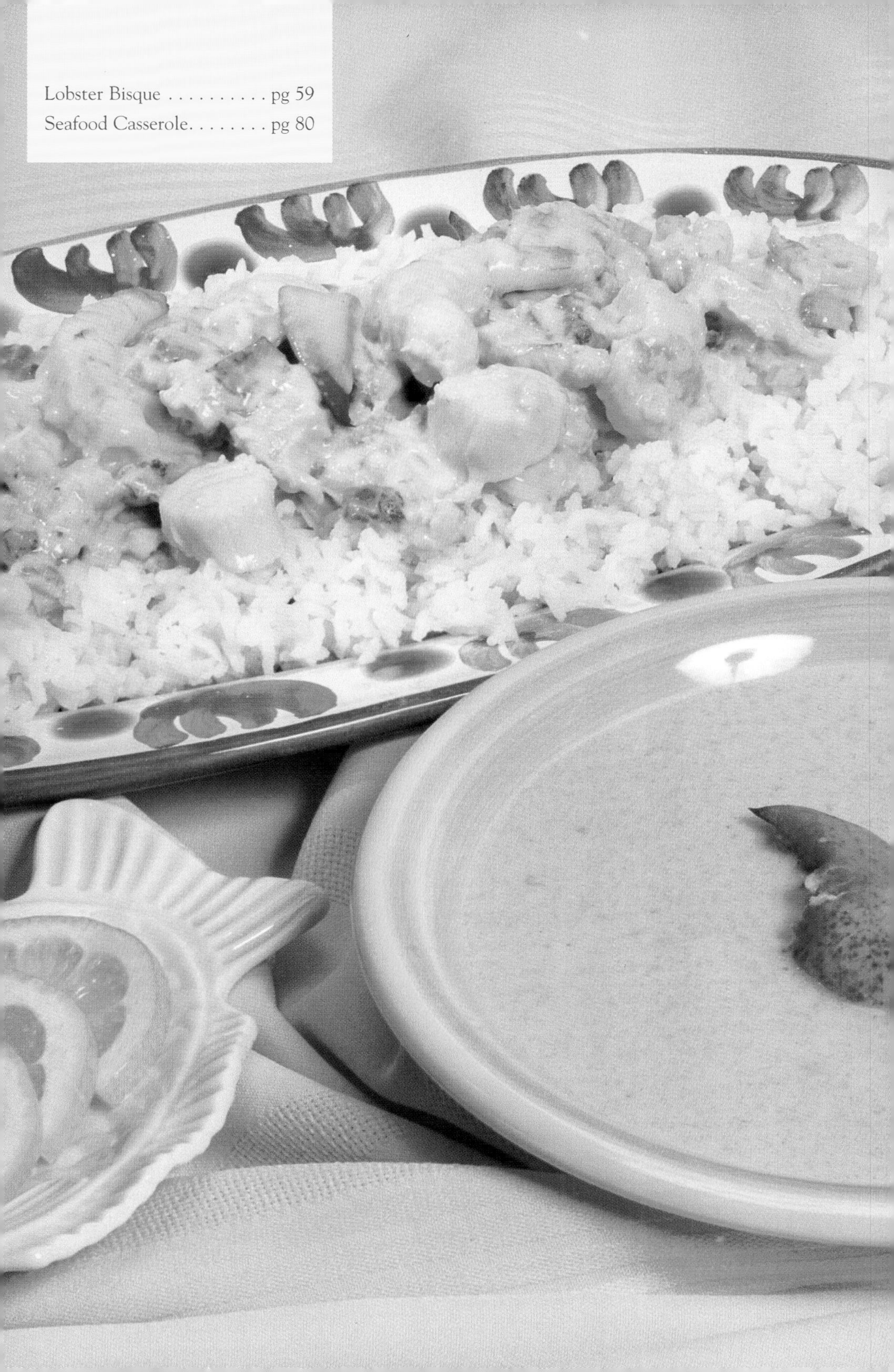

Sante Fe Style Barbeque Salmon

This recipe combines the spicy sweet flavours of the south with the delicate flavour of Pacific Salmon.

6 - 8	salmon steaks	6 - 8

MARINADE

1	garlic clove, minced	1
1	jalapeno pepper , finely sliced	1
1	onion, finely chopped	1
1/2 cup	lime juice	125 mL
1/2 cup	McCain's Orange Juice	125 mL
1/2 cup	olive oil	125 mL
2 tsp	Dijon mustard	10 mL
1 tsp	salt	5 mL
1 tsp	Tone's Ground Cumin	5 mL
1 tsp	sugar	5 mL

SALSA SAUCE

2	tomatillos, husked and chopped	3
4	green onions, finely chopped	4
1	large tomato, chopped	1
1 tsp	chopped fresh cilantro	5 mL
*1/4 cup	reserved marinade	50 mL

In a small bowl, combine garlic, jalapeno and onion. Add lime, McCain's Orange Juice and olive oil. Stir in mustard, salt, cumin, and sugar. Blend well. Reserve 1/4 cup (50 mL) marinade and place in refrigerator.

Place remaining marinade over salmon steaks in a non-metallic container with a tight fitting cover or place in a plastic bag. Marinate in the refrigerator for 1 to 2 hours. Prepare salsa sauce (see method below).

SALSA SAUCE

Remove dry outer husk from tomatillos. Wash. Chop into small cubes. In a small non-metallic bowl combine onion, tomatillo, tomato and cilantro.

Pour reserved marinade over salsa and gently toss. Refrigerate until serving. Serve as a garnish on salmon.

Remove steaks from marinade. Pat dry. Discard marinade. Barbecue over medium heat or broil for 5 minutes per inch of thickness. Transfer to serving platter. Garnish with salsa sauce.

Makes 6 - 8 servings.

Lobster Thermidor

An elegant appetizer for any special day.

2	tbsp	Alpha Butter	25	mL
1	cup	chopped mushrooms	250	mL
1	tbsp	finely chopped onion	15	mL
3	tbsp	Co-op Flour	45	mL
1/2	tsp	Tone's Dry Mustard	2	mL
1/4	tsp	Tone's Paprika	1	mL
1/2	tsp	salt	2	mL
Pinch		Tone's White Pepper	Pinch	
1 1/2	cups	Alpha Creamo	375	mL
2	cups	cooked lobster	500	mL
1/4	cup	shredded Armstrong Cheddar Cheese	50	mL

In a large saucepan melt butter, saute mushrooms and onion until onion is transparent, about 5 minutes. Sprinkle with flour, mustard, paprika, salt and pepper. Stir until combined.

Gradually add cream, stirring until thick and smooth. Add lobster and heat through.

Spoon into large scallop shells. Sprinkle with shredded cheese. Brown quickly under broiler.

Makes 6 servings.

Crispy Sole Fillets With Lemon Sauce

To reduce the fat leave out the butter from the lemon sauce.

1	lb	sole fillets	500 g
1/4	cup	Alpha Milk-2%	50 mL
1/3	cup	Robin Hood Oatbran	75 mL
1/2	cup	cornflake crumbs	125 mL
1	tsp	Tone's Dill Weed	5 mL
1/4	tsp	Tone's Lemon Pepper	1 mL
1/2	cup	Co-op Lemon Juice	125 mL
2	tbsp	sugar	25 mL
1	tbsp	cornstarch	15 mL
1/4	tsp	grated lemon peel	1 mL
1/2	tsp	Alpha Butter	2 mL

In a flat bottom bowl, place sole fillets. Pour milk over.

Combine oatbran, cornflake crumbs and lemon pepper. Dredge fillets in crumb mixture. Place on an ungreased baking sheet.

Bake in a 450° F (230° C) oven for 15 - 18 minutes until fish flakes easily.

In a small saucepan, combine Co-op Lemon Juice, sugar, cornstarch and lemon peel. Cook over medium heat until sauce is thick and clear. Stir constantly to prevent lumping. Remove from heat, stir in butter.

Arrange fillets on serving tray, pour lemon sauce over top and serve immediately.

Makes 3 - 4 servings.

Zesty Fish Steaks

Any firm fleshed fish (salmon, orange roughy, halibut, shark) is delicious when broiled after marinating.

	Grated peel of 1 lemon	
	Juice of 1 lemon	
1/4 cup	Co-op Soya Sauce	50 mL
2 tbsp	sugar	25 mL
1 tsp	Tone's Oregano	5 mL
1/2 tsp	Tone's Pepper	2 mL
1	clove garlic, minced	1
2 tbsp	chopped onion	25 mL
4	pieces (6 oz/400 g) fish steaks	4

In a shallow, non metallic, baking dish combine all ingredients except fish. Add fish to marinade. Marinate for 2 to 4 hours, any longer and the fish will become flaky and dry.

Place fish on a broiling pan and place on oven rack approximately 4 inches (10 cm) from the element. Baste with remaining marinade and broil for 5 minutes. Check for doneness by gently flaking with a fork, if fish flakes easily, it is done, or return to broiler just until cooked. Do not overcook.

Makes 4 servings.

Lemon Herb Halibut

A delicious, easy way to prepare fish.

1 lb	Halibut fish steaks	500	g
1/3 cup	bread crumbs	75	mL
1 tbsp	West Canola Oil	15	mL
2 tbsp	fresh parsley, chopped	25	mL
1 tsp	Tone's Dill Weed	5	mL
1/4 tsp	Tone's Pepper	1	mL
1 tsp	grated lemon rind	5	mL
2 tbsp	finely chopped onion	25	mL

Preheat oven to 450° F (230° C). In a shallow baking dish, arrange fish in a single layer. In a small bowl, combine crumbs, oil, parsley, dill, pepper, lemon rind and onion. Sprinkle mixture over fish. Bake uncovered for 10 minutes per inch of thickness for fish or until fish flakes easily when tested with a fork.

Makes 4 servings.

Saltimbocca Alla Romana

Include this wonderful entree to an Italian style dinner.

2 lbs	pork tenderloin	1 kg
8	thin slices prosciutto	8
1/2 lb	Armstrong Mozzarella Cheese, sliced	1/4 kg
	Tone's Sage	
	Tone's Parsley	
	minced garlic	
	Co-op Flour	
	olive oil to saute	
1/2 cup	dry white wine	125 mL

Cut pork into 16 - 1 inch (2.5 cm) thick pieces. Place meat cut side down. With a meat mallet pound to 1/8 inch (2 mm) thick (approximately 5 x 3 inches/12 x 8 cm). On top of each "scaloppini" place a slice of prosciutto, a slice of mozzarella, pinch of sage, pinch of parsley, and a little bit of the minced garlic. Place second "scaloppini" on top. Press edges together with a fork.

Dust each piece of meat with flour. In a large frying pan heat oil and saute meat until lightly browned. Place meat in a large casserole. Pour wine over meat. Bake at 350° F (180° C) for 1/2 hour.

Makes 8 servings.

Stuffed Pork Tenderloin

Procuitto is available from the Deli department. A winning recipe for the barbecue.

1 tbsp	olive oil	15 mL
1/2 cup	chopped onion	125 mL
1	clove garlic, minced	1
1/4 tsp	Tone's Sage	1 mL
1/4 tsp	Tone's Thyme	1 mL
Pinch	Tone's Pepper	Pinch
1	can (10 oz/284 mL) Co-op Chicken Broth	1
1/4 cup	Sunrype Apple Juice	50 mL
1/2 cup	dried fruit bits	125 mL
3/4 cup	corn meal	175 mL
2 tbsp	fresh parsley, chopped	25 mL
2 oz	procuitto, chopped fine	50 g
2	pork tenderloins	2

BASTING SAUCE

1/4 cup	Sunrype Blue Label Apple Juice	50 mL
2 tbsp	West Canola Oil	25 mL

In a large saucepan heat oil. Saute onion, garlic, sage, thyme and pepper until onions are transparent. Add chicken broth, apple juice and dried fruit bits. Bring to a boil. Boil for 1 minute. Stir in corn meal and continue to cook until thick and moisture is absorbed. Add parsley and procuitto and stir until combined.

Split tenderloins horizontally, do not cut all the way through. Lay the tenderloins open and pound to flatten slightly. Spread stuffing over tenderloins and roll closed. Secure roll closed with butcher string. In a small bowl combine 1/4 cup (50 mL) apple juice and oil. Heat barbeque to high, reduce heat to low then cook tenderloins on a greased grill for 40 minutes, occasionally turning and basting with apple mixture.

Makes 6 - 8 servings.

Parmesan Veal

Best if breaded and chilled before cooking. These thin veal cutlets quickly cook in a Parmesan crust to tender results.

1	Country Morning Egg	1	
1 tbsp	water	15	mL
1 cup	Alpha Grated Parmesan Cheese	250	mL
1/2 cup	fine bread crumbs	125	mL
1 tsp	seasoned pepper	5	mL
1 tsp	Tone's Basil	5	mL
6	fresh veal cutlets	6	
2 tbsp	olive oil	25	mL

In a shallow bowl beat together egg and water. In another shallow, wide bowl or plate combine cheese, bread crumbs, pepper and basil.

Dip cutlet into the egg wash. Then coat with crumb mixture. Loosely wrap with waxed paper and chill in refrigerator for at least 2 hours. In a large skillet heat olive oil, 1 tsp (5 mL) per cutlet and cook over medium high temperature until golden on each side and cooked through, about 5 - 7 minutes per side.

Makes 6 servings.

"Herb's" Lime Grilled Chicken

If fresh herbs are unavailable substitute half as much dried. Rub herbs between your hands to release the aromatic oils.

1/2 cup	fresh lime juice (2 large limes)	125 mL
1/4 cup	West Canola Oil	50 mL
2 tbsp	Co-op Honey	25 mL
1 tsp	fresh chopped thyme	5 mL
1 tsp	fresh chopped rosemary	5 mL
1	clove garlic, crushed	1
4	boned and skinned Country Morning Chicken Breasts	4

In a non-metallic medium sized container combine lime juice, oil, honey, thyme, rosemary and garlic. Whisk together until well blended.

Marinate chicken breasts in lime mixture for 1 to 2 hours in the refrigerator.

Place on a lightly greased broiling pan and grill basting once or twice in the first half of cooking time until chicken is cooked through.

Makes 4 servings.

Easy Oven Baked Chicken

This no fuss recipe will be enjoyed by adults and children alike.

1/2	cup	dried bread crumbs	125	mL
1/2	cup	grated Romano cheese	125	mL
1/4	tsp	Tone's Pepper	1	mL
1/4	tsp	Tone's Garlic Powder	1	mL
1/2	tsp	Tone's Italian Seasoning	2	mL
3	lbs	chicken pieces, skinned	1.5	kg
1	cup	Yoplait Light Plain Yogourt	250	mL

In a shallow bowl, combine crumbs, cheese, pepper, garlic powder and seasoning. Set aside. Dip chicken pieces into yogourt, then coat with crumb mixture. Shake off any excess crumbs. Arrange chicken on a baking tray and bake in a 375° F (190° C) oven for 40 minutes.

Makes 4 - 6 servings.

Tandoori Chicken

The spices enhance, but don't overpower this sumptuious dish.

1 tsp	Tone's Cumin Seeds	5	mL
1/2 tsp	Tone's Dill Seeds	2	mL
1	clove garlic, minced	1	
1 tsp	Tone's Dry Mustard	5	mL
1 tbsp	Tone's Coriander	15	mL
1 tsp	Tone's Pepper	5	mL
1 tsp	Tone's Ground Ginger	5	mL
1/4 cup	Co-op Lemon Juice	50	mL
1 tsp	salt	5	mL
1	cut up frying chicken, skinned	1	

Crush cumin and dill seeds in a mortar and pestle or crush well between waxed paper with a rolling pin. In a small bowl combine all spices with lemon juice. In a non-metallic bowl place chicken, pour in spice mixture, stir with chicken and close securely. Place container in refrigerator. Marinate for 1 - 24 hours.

Place chicken on grill over medium coals and barbecue 10 minutes per side or until cooked through. Alternately, grill under broiler for 7 minutes per side.

Makes 4 servings.

Stuffed Chicken Breasts

Boneless chicken breasts stuffed with Stilton cheese are simmered in an aromatic onion and sherry sauce.

2	whole boneless Country Morning Chicken Breasts, skinned	2
2 oz	Stilton cheese	50 g
2 tsp	West Canola Oil	10 mL
1 cup	finely chopped onion	250 mL
1	clove garlic, minced	1
1/2 tsp	Tone's Pepper	2 mL
1	can (10 oz/284 mL) Co-op Chicken Broth	1
1/2 cup	sherry	125 mL
	Hot cooked rice	

Halve chicken breasts, carefully cut a side pocket into each chicken piece. Evenly divide cheese into 4 pieces, insert a piece of cheese into each chicken pocket. Heat oil over medium high heat and cook chicken five minutes on each side. Transfer chicken to a plate. In the same skillet saute onion and garlic for five minutes. Add pepper, broth and sherry and cook until mixture has reduced to about 1 cup (250 mL). Return chicken to skillet and cook for 7 minutes, or until chicken is no longer pink inside. Serve with rice.

Makes 4 servings.

Spinach Parmesan Turnovers

These turnovers are great for lunch.
Thin chicken, veal, pork or turkey cutlets all work well to fold-over this tasty filling.

1/2 cup	cooked spinach	125 mL
1/4 cup	Alpha Grated Parmesan Cheese, divided	50 mL
1 tbsp	olive oil	15 mL
1 tbsp	Co-op Chopped Pecans or Pine Nuts	15 mL
1	clove garlic, minced	1
1 tsp	Tone's Basil	5 mL
4	turkey cutlets	4
1	Country Morning Egg	1
2 tbsp	water	25 mL
1/2 cup	fine bread crumbs	125 mL

In a blender or food processor whir together spinach, 2 tbsp (25 mL) cheese, oil, nuts, garlic and basil, just until blended.

On a plate or plastic board place cutlet. Spread with 2 tbsp (25 mL) of the spinach puree. Fold over to make a turnover. Repeat with remaining cutlets.

Whisk egg with water. Dip folded cutlet in egg and roll in bread crumbs combined with remaining Parmesan cheese. Place breaded turnovers on a cookie sheet. Bake in a 350° F (180° C) oven for 20 - 25 minutes until juices run clear. Cool and refrigerate until ready to use. These also freeze well.

Makes 4 servings.

Chicken Mole

Nuns In Pueblo were supposed to have created this dish for a visiting dignitary. They put everything in the kitchen into the sauce, which has become a national feast dish. Chocolate and banana sweeten this spicy concoction. There are as many mole recipes as there are chickens in Mexico.

2	lbs	chicken pieces	1	kg
2	cups	prepared Knorr Instant Chicken Stock	500	mL
2	tbsp	Tone's Chili Powder	25	mL
1/2	cup	Co-op Ground Almonds	125	mL
1		small chopped banana	1	
2	tbsp	Tone's Sesame Seeds	25	mL
2		green onion	2	
4		cloves garlic, minced	4	
1	tsp	Tone's Cinnamon	5	mL
1		can (4 oz/114 mL) chopped mild green chilies	1	
2		corn tortillas, torn	2	
1		square (1 oz/28 g) semi sweet chocolate	1	
2	tbsp	Alpha Butter	25	mL

Remove skin from chicken pieces. In a larger skillet simmer pieces in chicken broth until done. Remove pieces and keep warm, reserve hot broth.

To prepare sauce: In a blender or food processor whir together until very smooth chili powder, almonds, banana, sesame seeds, green onion, garlic, cinnamon, tomato paste, reserved broth and torn corn tortillas. Transfer to skillet and heat to simmer, add semi sweet chocolate and butter and stir until melted. Add chicken pieces and simmer in mole until warmed through. Serve hot.

Makes 6 servings.

Alberta Beef in Beer Sauce

Ask the Co-op butcher to cut these steaks extra thick. Place in marinade a couple of hours before cooking to allow flavours to develop.

2	2 inch (10 cm) thick sirloin steaks	2

MARINADE

1	can (375 mL) non-alcoholic beer	1
1	can (10 oz/284 mL) Co-op Beef Broth	1
1 1/2 tsp	sugar	7 mL
1 tbsp	Co-op Vinegar	5 mL
1/4 cup	finely chopped onion	50 mL
1 tsp	garlic, minced	5 mL
1 tsp	Tone's Thyme	5 mL
	Salt	
	Tone's Pepper	

Place marinade ingredients in a large plastic bag or bowl with a cover. Add steaks and marinate for 2 hours or overnight.

Remove steaks. Discard marinade.

Place steak on pre-heated medium high grill. Cook on high for 7 - 9 minutes per side for medium rare. Season with salt and pepper if desired. Transfer to platter. Cut across grain.

Serve immediately.

Makes 6 servings.

Pulled Beef

A strange name that makes sense when you start to pull or shred this tender simmered beef apart to pile onto fresh buns with lots of tangy sauce.
A nice touch for less tender beef cuts.

2 lbs	boneless cross rib, blade or rump steak	1 kg
	(approx. 2 inch (5 cm) thick)	
1 tsp	Dijon mustard	5 mL
2	cloves garlic, minced	2
1/4 tsp	liquid smoke	1 mL
1 tsp	Tone's Cajun Seasoning	5 mL
	Aluminum foil	
	Barbecue sauce (page 152)	
	Submarine style buns	

Dry off meat with paper towelling. In a small bowl make a paste of the mustard, garlic, liquid smoke and seasoning. Spread evenly over entire steak.

Wrap steak tightly in foil and place in a shallow pan. Roast in a 325° F (160° C) oven for 2 1/2 to 3 hours. Meat will "pull" away or shred easily with a fork. Serve meat on warm soft buns with lots of barbecue sauce.

Makes 4 - 6 servings.

Mr. Hay's Roast

A tribute to Bill Hay, for this wonderful barbecue recipe!

1	Boneless Top Round Steak, (2 inches/5 cm thick)	1	
1 1/2 cups	West Canola Oil	375	mL
3/4 cup	Co-op Soya Sauce	175	mL
1/4 cup	Worcestershire sauce	50	mL
2 tbsp	Tone's Dry Mustard	25	mL
2 tbsp	salt	25	mL
1 tbsp	Tone's Pepper	15	mL
1/2 cup	red wine vinegar	125	mL
1 1/2 tsp	Tone's Parsley	7	mL
2	garlic cloves, minced	2	
1/3 cup	fresh Co-op Lemon Juice	75	mL

Pierce steak repeatedly on both sides with fork.

In a bowl, combine remaining ingredients. Mix well. Marinate steak in a non-aluminum pan 24 - 48 hours in the refrigerator, turning 2 to 3 times.

Grill steak over medium hot coals, turning every 10 minutes and basting with each turn. The steak will take about 30 minutes for medium.

Discard leftover marinade.

Thinly slice across the grain.

Makes 10 servings.

Micro Meatloaf

A round pan with the centre removed, such as a microwave proof bundt pan,
(or use a round cake dish with a centre made from an inverted small pyrex cup),
will help ensure even cooking.

1 lb	lean ground beef	500 g
1	Country Morning Egg	1
3/4 cup	Co-op Herb Seasoned Croutons	175 mL
1/4 cup	Alpha Milk-2%	50 mL
1/2 cup	diced Swiss cheese	125 mL
2 tbsp	Co-op Ketchup	25 mL
1 tbsp	Knorr Instant Beef Stock	15 mL
2 tbsp	Co-op Soya Sauce	25 mL

In a large mixing bowl toss together ground beef and remaining ingredients until combined. Gently press into a bundt style microwave proof pan. Cook on MEDIUM or 50% power for 12 - 14 minutes. Turning 3 times throughout cooking if not on a turntable. Let stand for 5 minutes before serving.

Makes 4 servings.

Mini Mango Meat Muffins

This spicy little meat "muffin" only needs some steamed snow peas for a complete meal.
Too much mixing will make the "muffins" tough.

1 lb	ground beef	500 g
1/4 cup	Co-op Rice	50 mL
1/4 cup	mango chutney	50 mL
1 tsp	Tone's Curry Powder	5 mL
1/2 cup	finely chopped onion	125 mL
1	can (10 oz/284 mL) Co-op Beef Broth	1

In a medium bowl, lightly combine ground beef, rice, chutney, curry powder and onion. Add half can of beef broth - stir lightly.

Divide mixture into 4 mini loaf pans or divide evenly between 4 or 6 deep muffin tins. Evenly divide remaining broth over top.

Place in 425° F (220° C) oven for 35 - 40 minutes.

Makes 4 servings.

Tender Beef Brisket

The result is a juicy, fork tender piece of beef.

5 lb	lean, flat brisket of beef	2.5 kg
1 tsp	seasoning salt	5 mL
1 tsp	Tone's Lemon Pepper	5 mL
3	garlic cloves, minced	3
6	large carrots, pared and sliced	6
2	medium onions, cut into wedges	2
4	large celery stalks, sliced	4
1	can (10 oz/284 mL) Co-op Beef Broth	1
1 1/4 cup	water	300 mL
1/2 cup	red wine	125 mL

Preheat oven to 325° F (160° C). Rub brisket with seasoning salt and pepper.

Place garlic, carrots, onions and celery on bottom of roasting pan. Place flat brisket on top of vegetables and add beef broth, water and red wine.

Cover and roast for 3 1/2 - 4 hours. This long, moist cooking method is required to tenderize the meat.

Transfer beef to serving platter; cover and keep warm. Skim off fat from broth and vegetables. Broth and vegetables may be served as is or process them together in a food processor to make a smooth gravy. Slice beef and serve.

Makes 6 - 8 servings.

Reuben Rouladens

Look for beef rouladens at the meat counter. If not available purchase beef top round steak and pound to 1/4 inch (1/2 cm) thickness.

1	lb	beef rouladens	500	g
2	tbsp	coarse mustard	25	mL
1		can (14 oz/398 mL) sauerkraut, drained	1	
1	cup	grated Swiss cheese	250	mL

Unroll rouladens. Spread each with coarse mustard. Cut in half. Rinse and drain sauerkraut. Divide sauerkraut and spread evenly on each piece of meat. Sprinkle 2 tbsp (25 mL) grated Swiss cheese on each. Roll up jelly roll style. Place rolls, seam side down on a shallow roasting pan.

Roast uncovered in 400° F (200° C) oven for 25 minutes.

Serve immediately with buttered noodles or potatoes and green beans.

Makes 4 servings.

Sate Burger

Believe it or not Peanut Butter and Burgers is a winning combo.

2 lbs	ground beef	1	kg
1	bunch, green onions, sliced	1	
2	cloves garlic, minced	2	
1 tbsp	Worcestershire sauce	15	mL
1 tsp	Co-op Prepared Mustard	5	mL
1/4 tsp	hot pepper sauce	1	mL
1/2 tsp	Tone's Pepper	2	mL
8	Co-op Whole Wheat Hamburger Buns	8	

SATE SAUCE

1/3 cup	Co-op Peanut Butter	75	mL
2 tbsp	Hoisin sauce	25	mL
1 tbsp	Co-op Honey	15	mL
1 tbsp	West Canola Oil	15	mL
1 tsp	Tone's Ground Ginger	5	mL
1/4 tsp	Tone's Crushed Dry Chilies	1	mL
	Thinly sliced cucumber		

In a large mixing bowl, lightly break up ground beef. In a smaller bowl, combine green onions, garlic, Worcestershire, mustard, hot pepper sauce and pepper. Toss into ground beef, mixing lightly. Form into 8 - 1 inch (2.5 cm) thick patties.

Grill on medium high grill for 6 minutes per side. During the final 2 or 3 minutes of grilling, baste with Sate sauce.

SAUCE

In a saucepan combine peanut butter, Hoisin sauce, honey, oil, ginger and chilies. Heat. Stir over medium temperature until warm and saucy. Brush over burgers. Use remaining sauce to top cooked burgers.

Serve on whole wheat buns with thinly sliced cucumber.

Makes 8 hamburgers.

Tripoli Burger

The combination is Italian and Spicy.

2	lbs	ground beef	1	kg
1/2	cup	sliced black olives	125	mL
1/2	cup	sliced green olives	125	mL
1/4	cup	grated onion	50	mL
1/2	cup	Alpha Grated Parmesan Cheese	125	mL
1/4	cup	finely chopped red pepper	50	mL
1		Country Morning Egg	1	
1	tsp	Tone's Italian Seasoning	5	mL
8		split and toasted Kaiser Rolls	8	
8		slices Armstrong Mozzarella Cheese	8	
1		can (8 oz/227 mL) pizza sauce	1	

In a large mixing bowl gently break up ground beef. Add olives, onions, cheese and red pepper. In a small bowl, beat egg. Pour over meat mixture and toss ingredients together lightly until just combined.

Shape into 8 - 1 inch (2.5 cm) thick patties. Grill over medium high temperature 6 minutes per side until done. Baste with pizza sauce during last 2 minutes of cooking. Just before removing from grill, top with cheese and continue cooking until just melted.

Serve on toasted Kaiser Rolls.

Makes 8 hamburgers.

Jalapeno Cheese Rice

Jalapeno cheese is available in the cheese section of the dairy case.

3 cups	cooked Co-op Rice	750	mL
2 cups	Beatrice Sour Cream	500	mL
1 cup	shredded jalapeno cheese	250	mL
1 cup	sliced black or green olives	250	mL
1/2 cup	chopped fresh parsley	125	mL

In a (3 L) oven proof casserole dish stir together rice, sour cream, cheese, olives and parsley. Smooth top. Bake in a 350° F (180° C) oven for 40 minutes until bubbly.

Makes 6 servings.

Fresh Tomato Risotto

Short grain pearl rice, Italian style rice or Aborio simmer slowly in a rich broth.
The constant stirring produces a creamy full flavoured side dish or first course.

2 tbsp	olive oil	25 mL
1 cup	finely chopped onion	250 mL
2	cloves crushed garlic	2
1 1/2 cups	sliced mushrooms	375 mL
2 cups	Italian style rice	500 mL
3 cups	Knorr Instant Beef Stock, divided	750 mL
1 cup	finely chopped roma tomatoes	250 mL
1 tsp	Tone's Rosemary, crushed	5 mL
	Tone's Pepper	

In a large skillet over medium high, heat oil. Add onion, garlic and mushrooms. Saute until softened. Add rice and stir for about 3 minutes. Rice will brown slightly.

Meanwhile in another saucepan heat broth until simmering. Slowly add 1 cup (250 mL) broth to the rice mixture and stir slowly but constantly, allowing the rice to simmer. When the broth has been absorbed add another 1/2 cup (125 mL) and continue stirring until absorbed.

Continue adding broth 1/2 cup (125 mL) at a time until 2 1/2 cups (625 mL) has been absorbed.

Add the tomatoes and rosemary and remaining 1/2 cup broth, stirring constantly. Rice will be creamy and tender. All together the rice should cook 25 - 30 minutes. Serve immediately with fresh ground pepper.

Makes 6 servings.

Italian Style Potatoes

Pizza in a potato!

6		large potatoes, baked	6	
1/4	cup	finely chopped onion	50	mL
1		clove garlic, minced	1	
1	tbsp	West Canola Oil	15	mL
1	cup	Co-op Tomato Sauce	250	mL
1		green pepper, chopped	1	
1/2	tsp	Tone's Oregano	2	mL
1/2	tsp	Tone's Chili Powder	2	mL
1/2	lb	pepperoni sausage, chopped	250	g
1/2	cup	sliced black olives	125	mL
1	cup	shredded Armstrong Mozzarella Cheese	250	mL

Cut 1/3 off the top of the potatoes and scoop pulp into a bowl, leaving 1/2 inch (1 cm) of potato inside skin. Set aside.

In a medium size bowl, combine onion, garlic and oil. Microwave on high for two minutes. Add tomato sauce, green pepper, oregano, chili powder, pepperoni and half of the potato pulp. (Remaining potato can be added to soup or fried as hash browns). Cook on high for 3 - 4 minutes. Stir in olives and 1/2 cup (125 mL) of the Mozzarella. Cook on high for 30 seconds. Stuff each potato with filling mixture. Sprinkle remaining Mozzarella on top. Microwave 3 of the potatoes at a time. Cook on high for 3 minutes.

Makes 6 servings.

Spicy Bean Refry

As an accompaniment to a main course or a filler for tacos and tortillas. The canned refried beans are convenient and work for any recipe calling for "refries".

1	can (4 oz/114 mL) chopped mild green chilies	50 mL
1/2 cup	chopped onion	125 mL
1	clove garlic, crushed	1
1 tbsp	West Canola Oil	15 mL
2	cans (398 mL) refried beans	2
1 tsp	Tone's Ground Cumin	5 mL

In a heavy bottomed skillet, heat oil. Add chilies, onion and garlic. Saute until onions are transparent. Stir in beans and cumin and heat until simmering. Serve hot.

Makes 6 - 8 servings.

See photo page 121

Savoury Rice Pilaf

A herb flavoured side dish for chicken or pork. Use a pre-mixed combination of wild and brown rice, or all brown if preferred.

2	cans (10 oz/284 mL) Co-op Chicken Broth	2	
1 1/4 cup	wild and brown rice	300	mL
2 tbsp	olive oil	25	mL
1/2 cup	chopped onion	125	mL
1 cup	finely sliced celery	250	mL
1 cup	finely sliced mushrooms	250	mL
1/2 cup	chopped red pepper	125	mL
1/2 cup	sliced Co-op Almonds	125	mL
1/2 tsp	Tone's Thyme	2	mL
1/2 tsp	Tone's Sage	2	mL
1/4 tsp	Tone's Garlic Salt	1	mL

In a heavy saucepan with a lid bring broth to a boil. Add rice and reduce temperature to low. Cover and cook 20 - 25 minutes until liquid is absorbed. Remove from heat.

In a skillet heat olive oil. Add onion, celery, mushrooms, pepper and almonds, saute over medium heat until vegetables are tender. Stir in seasonings and cook 5 minutes. Stir in cooked rice.

Makes 4 - 6 servings.

Barley Stuffing

A hearty stuffing of barley and seasonal vegetables.

2 cups	uncooked Co-op Barley	500 mL
4	cans (10 oz/284 mL) Co-op Chicken Broth	4
1 lb	Country Morning Bacon	500 g
2	cloves garlic, minced	2
3 cups	chopped onion	750 mL
2 cups	sliced celery	500 mL
2 cups	chopped carrot	500 mL
1 cup	chopped tomato	250 mL
1 tsp	Tone's Poultry Seasoning	5 mL
	Tone's Pepper	

In a medium size saucepan over medium low heat, add barley and chicken broth. Cover and simmer about 1 hour until barley is cooked.

Cut bacon into 1 inch (2.5 cm) pieces.

In a fry pan, saute bacon until crisp. Add garlic, onion, celery, carrot and cook until tender crisp. Drain.

Add to barley. Add tomato and seasonings. Toss well. Spoon into turkey cavity. Place slice of bread over stuffing to seal off cavity.

Makes 6 cups (1.5 L).

Southern Cornmeal Stuffing

A popular stuffing in the Southern States. Makes double the quantity you need for your turkey - but the extra is delicious for brunch.

1/2 lb	Country Morning Sausage	250 g
1/2 cup	Alpha Butter	125 mL
1/4 cup	sugar	50 mL
4	Country Morning Eggs	4
1	can (4 oz/114 mL) chopped green chilies, drained	1
1	can (14 oz/398 mL) Co-op Cream Style Corn	1
1 cup	shredded Armstrong Monterey Jack Cheese	250 mL
1/4 cup	finely chopped onion	50 mL
1 cup	Co-op Flour	250 mL
1 cup	yellow cornmeal	250 mL
1 tbsp	Magic Baking Powder	15 mL

Cook sausage. Drain fat. Slice into thin rounds. Let cool.

In a medium bowl cream butter and sugar. Add eggs one at a time beating after each addition. Add chilies, corn, cheese, onion and sausage. Blend well.

Sift together flour, cornmeal and baking powder. Add to corn mixture.

Pour into 2 - 8 X 8 inch (2 L) baking pans. Place in a 325° F (160° C) oven for 45 minutes.

One pan will fill a 20 lb (9 kg) turkey.

Pasta Puttenesco

A very fast, very popular pasta sauce in Italy.

1 tbsp	olive oil	15 mL
1 cup	chopped onion	250 mL
1/2 cup	sliced olives	125 mL
1	zucchini, grated	1
3	cloves garlic, crushed	3
2 tbsp	capers	25 mL
1	can (14 oz/398 mL) crushed Co-op Tomatoes	1
1	can(14 oz/398 mL) Co-op Tomato Sauce	1
4 cups	cooked Catelli Pasta	1 L

In a skillet saute onion, olives, zucchini and garlic until onions are transparent.
Add capers, tomatoes and tomato sauce. Simmer 20 minutes. Serve over pasta.

Makes 4 servings.

See photo page 25

Colcannon

Potatoes play an essential part in the Irish diet.

6	medium potatoes, peeled	6
1/2	small head of cabbage, shredded	1/2
3	stalks green onion, finely chopped	3
1/4 cup	water	50 mL
1/2 cup	Alpha Milk-2%	125 mL
2 tbsp	Alpha Butter	25 mL
1/2 tsp	salt	2 mL
Pinch	Tone's Pepper	Pinch

Boil potatoes until tender. Drain. Set potatoes aside. In a large saucepan, place cabbage, green onions and water. Bring to a boil, reduce heat, cover and simmer for 5 minutes or until cabbage is tender crisp.

Meanwhile, mash potatoes, add in milk, butter, salt and pepper. Beat until potatoes are fluffy. Stir in cabbage mixture. Serve hot.

Makes 6 servings.

Lacy Potato Pancakes (Latkes)

Mountains of crisp latkes just disappear. Serve miniatures for hor d'oeuvres or larger ones with the main course.

4	medium potatoes, peeled	4
1	small onion	1
2	Country Morning Eggs	2
1/3 cup	Co-op Flour	75 mL
1 tsp	Magic Baking Powder	5 mL
3/4 tsp	salt	3 mL
Pinch	Tone's Lemon Pepper	Pinch
	West Canola Oil for frying	
	Beatrice Sour Cream	
	Sunrype Apple Sauce	

Coarsly grate peeled potatoes. Place potatoes in a colander and rinse under cold water to remove the starch. Drain well. Grate onion, removing any excess moisture by placing in colander and pressing with the back of a wooden spoon.

In a mixing bowl combine potato and onion. Beat eggs into mixture; stir in flour, baking powder, salt and pepper.

Heat a small amount of oil in a large skillet. For each pancake, drop about 2 tablespoons (25 mL) of batter into the oil and flatten with the back of a wooden spoon; the flatter the pancake, the crisper it will be. Brown on both sides. Drain well on paper towels. Keep the cooked pancakes warm in a low oven.

Serve with sour cream and apple sauce. May be made ahead of and refrigerated between layers of waxed paper when cooled. To reheat, place in a single layer on an ungreased cookie sheet. Bake, uncovered at 450° F (230° C) for 5 minutes, or until crisp and hot.

Makes about 2 dozen large or 5 dozen miniatures.

Corn Fritters

Lightly dusted with sugar and served with apple sauce these crispy corn morsels are a delightful breakfast or brunch item. For a savoury item, omit sugar from the batter and sprinkle with seasoning salt before serving.

2	cups	fresh cooked corn kernels	500	mL
2		Country Morning Eggs, beaten	2	
2	tbsp	West Canola Oil	25	mL
2	cups	Co-op Flour	500	mL
2	tsp	Magic Baking Powder	10	mL
1	tsp	salt	5	mL
1	tbsp	sugar	15	mL
4	cups	West Canola Oil for deep frying	1	L
		icing sugar		
		Sunrype Apple Sauce		

In a mixing bowl stir together corn, eggs and oil. Sift together dry ingredients and stir into corn mixture to form a soft batter.

Heat oil to 375° F (190° C) and drop batter by the tablespoon into the hot oil. Fry until puffed and golden, 3 to 4 minutes per fritter.

Drain on paper towelling and dust with icing sugar.

Serve warm with apple sauce.

Makes 15 - 18 fritters.

Zesty Zucchini Relish

This is a zippy relish you'll use frequently. Similar to the popular green hot dog relish.

14	medium zucchini (4 lbs/2 kg) quartered	14
5	medium onions (1 1/2 lbs/700 g) quartered	5
1	large sweet green pepper, seeded, quartered	1
1	large sweet red pepper, seeded and cut into small pieces	1
1/3 cup	pickling salt	75 mL
2 1/2 cups	sugar	625 mL
1 tsp	Tone's Nutmeg	5 mL
1 tsp	Tone's Turmeric	5 mL
2 1/2 cups	Co-op Vinegar	625 mL
4 tbsp	prepared horseradish	20 mL
1	large hot pepper, unseeded and finely chopped	1

Using a food processor fitted with metal blade, chop zucchini, onions and green pepper (to yield about 16 - 17 cups). Place in a large glass, stainless steel or enamel container. Stir in red pepper and pickling salt. Cover and let stand overnight.

Drain vegetables; rinse with cold water, then drain into cheesecloth lined colander, twisting cheesecloth to remove excess moisture.

Place vegetables in a large saucepan. Stir in remaining ingredients and bring to a boil. Reduce heat and simmer 45 minutes until thick.

Ladle relish into prepared hot jars to within 1/2 inch (1 cm) of top rim. Remove air bubbles.

Clean jar rims and threads.

Cover immediately with lids and screw bands.

Place in boiling water bath. Process for 15 minutes for pint jars.

Remove jars from water and cool.

Check seals when cool.

Makes 6 pint-size jars.

Zucchini Marmalade

Sounds unusual, but very tasty. The zucchini absorbs the citrus flavours for a superb spread.

2	lemons	2
1/3 cup	finely chopped peeled ginger root	75 mL
12 cups	grated zucchini	3 L
6 cups	sugar	1500 mL

Chop lemons and ginger, mix with zucchini (leave covered overnight to develop juices).

The next day place in a large Dutch Oven or heavy bottomed canner. Add sugar; bring to a boil. * Insert thermometer into centre of marmalade. Cook until mixtures reaches the temperature below. This will take approximately 1 1/2 - 2 hours.

Immediately ladle jam into hot sterilized jars to within 1/4 inch (5 mm) of top rim. Remove air bubbles by sliding a knife between the jar and jam.

Clean jar rim and threads.

Cover immediately with lids and screwbands.

Place in boiling water bath. Process 5 minutes.

Remove jars from water and cool.

Check seals when cool.

Makes 8 - 1/2 pint (250 mL) jars.

* Test the temperature water boils at on the day you are making your marmalade. Altitude causes variations in the boiling point of water. Add 9° F (6° C) to that temperature.

See photo page 42

Kiwi Daiquiri Jam

This is a sweet, but tart tasting jam with a subtle rum flavour. A festive treat.
Try it along side roast lamb.

10	kiwi fruit, peeled	10
6 cups	sugar	1500 mL
1 1/3 cups	Co-op Unsweetened Pineapple Juice	300 mL
2/3 cup	fresh lime juice	150 mL
2	pouches liquid pectin	2
1/2 cup	white rum	125 mL

In a large saucepan, mash kiwi fruit; stir in sugar, pineapple juice and lime juice.

Bring mixture to a full rolling boil, stirring until sugar dissolves. Boil vigorously for 1 minute; stirring constantly.

Remove from heat; stir in pectin. Continue stirring 5 minutes to prevent floating fruit. Stir in rum.

Immediately ladle jam into hot sterilized jars to within 1/4 inch (5 mm) of top rim. Clean jar rim and threads.

Cover immediately with lids and screwbands.

Place in boiling water bath. Process 5 minutes.

Remove jars from water and cool.

Invert jars after 2 hours to suspend fruit.

Check seals when cool.

Makes 8 - 1/2 pint (250 mL) size jars.

Strawberry Cointreau Jam

The flavour of summer strawberries are revisited all winter when eating this jam.

4 cups	strawberries	1 L
3 cups	sugar	750 mL
1/4 cup	Co-op Lemon Juice	50 mL
1/4 cup	Cointreau (optional)	50 mL

Layer strawberries and sugar in a Dutch Oven - let stand for 2 hours. Crush strawberries with potato masher. Over medium high heat bring mixture to full rolling boil. Boil for 5 minutes. Stir occasionally. Add lemon juice. Continue boiling for 5 more minutes. Remove from heat. Add Cointreau. Skim off any foam.

Ladle into hot sterilized jars to 1/4 inch (5 mm) from top rim. Clean jar rim and threads. Cover immediately with lids and screwbands. Place in boiling water bath and process for 15 minutes.

Remove jars from water and cool.

Check seals when cool.

Makes 3 - 4 1/2 pint (250 mL) jars.

Tomato Salsa Fiesta

A fresh and vibrant condiment for Mexican foods, or a chicken and burger topping!

4		large tomatoes, peeled	4
2		cloves garlic, chopped finely	2
1	tbsp	lime juice	15 mL
1/2	tsp	Tone's Cumin	2 mL
1/2	tsp	salt	2 mL
2	tbsp	West Canola Oil	25 mL
1	cup	diced red onion (about 1 medium)	250 mL
2	tbsp	chopped, fresh cilantro or parsley	25 mL
1		whole jalapeno pepper (seeds removed), chopped finely	1

Peel tomatoes by blanching 1 minute and cooling in ice water 1 minute. Dice tomatoes or chop one at a time in the food processor.

Combine garlic, lime juice, cumin and salt; beat in oil. Gently toss with remaining ingredients. Marinate at room temperature for 1 hour or several hours in the refrigerator.

Makes about 3 cups (750 mL).

Salsa

A great dip to serve with crackers, corn chips or vegetables.

7	lbs	tomatoes (approximately 30)	3	kg
2	cups	finely chopped celery	500	mL
2		large green peppers, finely chopped	2	
2		large sweet red peppers, chopped	2	
2	cups	chopped onion	500	mL
1		small red chili, seeded and chopped	1	
2		large mild jalapeno, chopped finely with seeds	2	
5		cloves garlic, minced	5	
1		can (114 mL/4 oz) green chilies, drained and chopped	1	
1		can (369 mL/ 13 oz) Co-op Tomato Paste	1	
2-3		drops hot pepper sauce	2-3	
3/4	cup	Co-op Vinegar	175	mL
2	tbsp	sugar	25	mL
1	tbsp	pickling salt	15	mL
2	tsp	Tone's Paprika	10	mL
1/4	cup	chopped fresh cilantro leaves or fresh parsley	50	mL

Blanch tomatoes in boiling water; rinse in cold water; remove peels.

Coarsely chop tomatoes. Place tomatoes in a large heavy saucepan.

Add all remaining ingredients. Simmer for 1/2 hour.

Ladle sauce into prepared pint (500 mL) jars, filling to 1/2 inch (5 mm) from top.

Clean jar rims and threads.

Cover immediately with lids and screw bands.

Place in boiling water bath. Process for 20 minutes for half pint (250 mL) jars; 25 minutes for pint (500 mL) jars.

Remove jars from water and cool. Check seals.

Makes 8 jars.

Barbeque Sauce

This is a mildly spicy barbecue sauce to use on any type of meat. Makes a nice gift for the outdoor cook.

6 lbs (about 24 large) peeled, cored, chopped ripe tomatoes	3 kg
2 cups	chopped celery	500 mL
2 cups	chopped onion	500 mL
1 1/2 cups	chopped sweet red or green peppers (about 3 med.)	375 mL
1	hot, red pepper, cored, chopped	1
1 tsp	Tone's Black Peppercorns	5 mL
2	cloves garlic, crushed	2
1 cup	brown sugar	250 mL
1	can (369 mL/13 oz) Co-op Tomato Paste	1
1 tbsp	Tone's Dry Mustard	15 mL
1 tbsp	Tone's Paprika	15 mL
1 tbsp	salt	15 mL
1 tsp	hot pepper sauce	5 mL
1/4 tsp	Tone's Cayenne Pepper	1 mL
1 cup	Co-op Vinegar	250 mL

In a Dutch Oven combine tomatoes, onions, celery and peppers. Simmer over medium heat until vegetables are soft, about 30 minutes. Stirring often.

Puree mixture using a food processor or blender.

Tie peppercorns in a cheesecloth bag. Add with remaining ingredients and simmer, stirring frequently, for 1/2 hour or until mixture thickens and is smooth. Remove bag of peppercorns.

Ladle hot sauce into hot sterilized pint-size (250 mL) jars, filling 1/2 inch (1 cm) from the top.

Clean jar rims and threads.

Cover immediately with lids and screw bands.

Place in boiling water bath. Process 15 minutes.

Remove jars from water and cool.

Check seals when cool.

Makes 8 pint jars.

Blueberry Wine Vinegar

In any chicken recipe calling for wine, substitute half of the wine with blueberry vinegar and garnish dish with blueberries .... delicious.

4 cups	white wine vinegar	1 L
3 cups	blueberries, (divided) fresh or frozen (no syrup)	750 mL
1/2 tsp	Tone's Cinnamon	2 mL

In a large saucepan combine vinegar, 2 cups (500 mL) blueberries and cinnamon. Bring to a boil. Boil 2 minutes. Strain through cheesecloth. Place remaining blueberries into 4 bottles. Fill with vinegar. Close tightly. Ready to use.

Raspberry Wine Vinegar

A wonderful change to spark up salads.

8 cups	red wine vinegar	2 L
4 cups	raspberries, fresh or frozen (no syrup)	1 L
1 cup	raspberries	250 mL

In a large saucepan heat red wine vinegar just until boiling. Place 4 cups (1 L) of raspberries in a large jar or container with tight fitting lid. Pour vinegar over raspberries. Replace lid and leave in a sunny window turning daily for 2 weeks. Strain and discard raspberries.

Reheat vinegar to just about boiling.

Divide 1 cup (250 mL) raspberries evenly into 4 - 6 clean bottles. Pour vinegar into bottles, close tightly. Ready to use.

The number of the bottles will vary depending on the sizes you have found.

Antipasto

It is very important to follow safe food handling for antipasto. You must process in a pressure canner or freeze the antipasto in canning jars or freezer containers. We recommend using pint or half pint containers to avoid having unused portions left over. Refrigerate any unserved portions left in the jar, for no more than two weeks.

* Note; anchovy paste can be found in the Dairy section.

1 lb	green peppers	450 g
1 lb	red peppers	450 g
1	cauliflower head (about 1 3/4 lb/800 g)	1
1	jar (24 oz/750 mL) dill pickles, drained	1
1	can (14 oz/398 mL) Co-op Green Beans, drained	1
1	can (14 oz/398 mL) Co-op Yellow Beans, drained	1
1	can (13 oz/375 mL) Co-op Green Stuffed Olives, drained	1
1	can (13 oz/375 mL) black pitted olives, drained	1
1	jar (24 oz/750 mL) pickled onions, drained	1
1	jar (32 oz/1 L) Co-op Ketchup	1
1 cup	olive oil	250 mL
1	tube (45 g) anchovy paste (optional)	1
1 cup	Co-op Vinegar	250 mL
4	cans (198 g) Co-op Solid White Tuna	4
1	can (10 oz/284 mL) Co-op Sliced Mushrooms, drained	1

Cut peppers in half and remove stems and seeds. Chop peppers, cauliflower, pickles, beans, olives and onions into small bite size pieces. In a very large stainless steel or enamel canning kettle, combine ketchup, olive oil, anchovy paste and vinegar. Flake tuna. Add tuna, mushrooms and chopped vegetables to pot. Bring to a boil and simmer for 10 minutes.

Ladle antipasto into sterilized jars, leaving 1/2 inch (1 cm) headspace. Remove air bubbles by sliding a knife between glass and food.

Wipe rim with a clean cloth. Center lid on jar and apply screw band just until finger tip tight. Place jars in canner.

Process in a pressure canner for 45 minutes at 12 - 15 lbs pressure or freeze.

Yield: 12 pint jars.

Three Fruit Chutney

This delicious chutney is wonderful served over cream cheese as an appetizer or as an accompaniment to bacon and eggs.

4	cups	sliced peeled peaches	1	L
2	cups	chopped plums	500	mL
2	cups	chopped tart apples	500	mL
1	cup	Co-op Raisins	250	mL
1		large onion, chopped	1	
1		lemon, thinly sliced and halved	1	
2	cups	brown sugar	500	mL
2	cups	cider vinegar	500	mL
1	tsp	salt	5	mL
1	tsp	Tone's Ground Ginger	5	mL
1	tsp	Tone's Whole Cloves	5	mL
1/2	tsp	Tone's Cinnamon	2	mL
1/2	tsp	Tone's Cayenne Pepper	2	mL

In a large Dutch Oven or preserving kettle combine all ingredients. Bring to a boil then reduce heat to medium and simmer for 1 1/2 hours or until thick. Ladle into hot sterilized jars leaving 1/4 inch (1 cm) headspace. Remove air bubbles by sliding a knife around glass and contents.

Wipe rim with a clean cloth.

Cover immediately with lids and screw bands.

Place in a boiling water bath. Process 15 minutes.

Makes approximately 8 - 1 cup (250 mL) jars.

Freezer Corn Relish

A hot dog's best friend, no other condiment needed. Equally wonderful served with roast pork or ham.

3 cups	uncooked fresh corn kernels (about 6 ears)	750 mL
1-1 1/2 cups	chopped onions	250-375 mL
1 cup	chopped celery	250 mL
1	red pepper, chopped	1
2 cups	cider vinegar	500 mL
1 cup	granulated sugar	250 mL
1 tbsp	Co-op Flour	15 mL
2 tsp	salt	10 mL
1 tsp	Tone's Celery Seeds	5 mL
1/2 tsp	Tone's Turmeric	2 mL

In preserving kettle or large non-aluminum saucepan, combine all ingredients. Mix well. Bring slowly to boil; simmer, uncovered for 30 to 40 minutes or until thickened.

Pack into hot sterilized jars, leaving 1/2 inch (1 cm) headspace, and seal. Let cool completely. Store in freezer for up to 1 year.

Makes 6 - 8 cups (1.5 to 2 L).

Citrus Cranberry Sauce

Wonderful over pancakes. Use as a basting sauce when grilling chicken or pork.

4 cups	Co-op Cranberry Juice	1 L
5 cups	sugar	1250 mL
2	small oranges, finely sliced	2
2 tbsp	Co-op Lemon Juice	25 mL
1	bottle liquid pectin	1
2 tbsp	finely chopped, candied ginger	25 mL

In a large saucepan combine cranberry juice, sugar, oranges and lemon juice. Over medium heat stir until all sugar is dissolved. Boil for 1 minute. Stir in pectin. Bring mixture back to a boil and boil hard for 2 minutes, stirring constantly. Remove from heat and skim off any foam. Stir in ginger.

Pour into sterilized jars. Place lids and screws. Process in a boiling water bath for 5 minutes.

Makes 6 - 1 cup (250 mL) jars.

Fruit Filled
Oatmeal Cookies

FILLING

1/2 cup	dried fruit (mixed, apricots, dates, etc.)	125 mL
1 cup	chopped peeled apples	250 mL
1/2 cup	Sunrype Apple Juice	125 mL
1/2 cup	sugar	125 mL
1/4 tsp	Tone's Cinnamon	1 mL
1 tbsp	Co-op Lemon Juice	15 mL

In a small saucepan combine fruit, apples and water. Cook until soft. Add sugar and cinnamon and cook until thick (15 - 20 minutes). Add lemon juice, stir. Let stand to cool.

COOKIES

1/3 cup	Alpha Butter	75 mL
1 cup	packed brown sugar	250 mL
1	Country Morning Egg	1
1/2 cup	Alpha Milk-2%	125 mL
1 tsp	Co-op Vanilla	5 mL
1/2 tsp	Co-op Almond Extract	2 mL
1 1/2 cups	Co-op Whole Wheat Flour	375 mL
1 tsp	Magic Baking Powder	5 mL
1/2 tsp	Co-op Baking Soda	2 mL
1 1/4 cups	Robin Hood Rolled Oats	300 mL
1/4 cup	wheat germ	50 mL
1/2 tsp	Tone's Cinnamon	2 mL
1 cup	Co-op Dried Apricots, chopped	250 mL

In a large mixing bowl cream together butter and sugar. Add egg; beat well. Beat in milk, vanilla and almond extract. Mix together flour, baking powder, baking soda, rolled oats, wheat germ, cinnamon and apricots. Stir into butter mixture. On a floured board, roll dough to 1/4 inch (1/2 cm) thickness. Cut into 3 1/2 inches (9 cm) circles. Place 1 tsp (5 mL) filling on circle. Fold over, seal edges.

Bake in a 375° F (190° C) oven for 12 - 15 minutes.

Makes 18 - 20 cookies.

Coffee Crumb Cake

This rich coffee flavoured crumb cake is wonderful served warm.

TOPPING

1/3 cup	Alpha Butter, softened	75 mL
1/4 cup	brown sugar	50 mL
1/3 cup	Co-op Flour	75 mL
1/2 cup	Robin Hood Rolled Oats	125 mL
1 tsp	Tone's Cinnamon	5 mL

CAKE

1/2 cup	Alpha Butter, softened	125 mL
1 cup	sugar	250 mL
2	Country Morning Eggs	2
2 cups	Co-op Flour	500 mL
1 tsp	Magic Baking Powder	5 mL
1 tsp	Co-op Baking Soda	5 mL
1/2 tsp	salt	2 mL
1 cup	Yoplait Low Fat Plain Yogourt	250 mL
1/2 cup	hot water	125 mL
4 tsp	Co-op Instant Coffee Granules	20 mL

TOPPING

Cream together butter and sugar. Add dry ingredients and blend until mixture is crumbly. Set aside.

CAKE

Preheat oven to 350° F (180° C). In a large bowl, cream together butter and sugar. Add eggs and vanilla and beat for 1 minute. In a separate bowl sift together flour, baking powder, soda and salt. Set aside.

In a third bowl dissolve coffee into water. Combine with yogourt. Add flour mixture and yogourt mixture alternately to creamed mixture. Beat in between additions. Spread batter in a greased 12 X 8 inch (20 X 30 cm) pan. Sprinkle with topping. Bake for 35 - 40 minutes. Serve warm.

See photo page 10

Lemon Poppy Seed Pound Cake

This moist cake tastes even better after "mellowing" for a day.

3/4 cup	Alpha Butter	175 mL
3/4 cup	sugar	175 mL
2	Country Morning Eggs	2
1 1/4 cups	sifted cake flour	300 mL
1 tsp	Magic Baking Powder	5 mL
1/4 tsp	salt	1 mL
2 tbsp	poppy seeds	25 mL
1/4 cup	Alpha milk-2%	50 mL
1 tsp	Co-op Vanilla	5 mL
2 tsp	grated lemon rind	10 mL

SYRUP

1/4 cup	sugar	50 mL
1/4 cup	Co-op Lemon Juice	50 mL

Preheat oven to 350° F (180° C). In a medium bowl, cream together butter and sugar. Add eggs, one at a time, beating well after each addition.

Sift together flour, baking powder and salt. Add poppy seeds and set aside.

Mix together milk, vanilla and lemon rind. Add the dry ingredients alternately with the liquids to the butter mixture, beating after each addition. Pour batter into a greased 4 X 8 inch (1.5 L) loaf pan. Bake 55 - 60 minutes or until a wooden toothpick inserted in the centre of the cake comes out clean.

SYRUP

Prepare syrup just before cake is finished baking. In a small pan, over medium heat, combine sugar and lemon juice until dissolved. Take warm cake and poke all over with a toothpick. Brush with 1/2 the syrup. Cool for five minutes then invert cake onto a rack. Poke cake bottom with toothpick and brush with remaining syrup. Cool and wrap air tight.

Makes 1 loaf.

Breakfast Cookie

These are "sturdy" cookies for breakfast on the go that will give you staying power all morning long.

1/2 cup	West Canola Oil	125 mL
1/2 cup	Co-op Peanut Butter	125 mL
1/2 cup	Co-op Honey	125 mL
1 cup	brown sugar	250 mL
2	Country Morning Eggs	2
1 tsp	Co-op Vanilla	5 mL
1 cup	Co-op Whole Wheat Flour	250 mL
1 tsp	salt	5 mL
1/2 tsp	Co-op Baking Soda	2 mL
3 cups	Robin Hood Rolled Oats	750 mL
1 cup	Co-op Unsweetened Coconut	250 mL
1/2 cup	bran	125 mL
1/4 cup	wheat germ	50 mL
1/2 cup	Robin Hood Oat Bran	125 mL
1 cup	Co-op Raisins	250 mL
1/2 cup	chopped Co-op Peanuts	125 mL

In a large mixing bowl cream together oil, peanut butter, honey and sugar. Add eggs and vanilla. Beat well. Stir in flour, salt and soda. Add remaining ingredients and stir well.

Drop by teaspoon (5 mL) onto a greased cookie sheet. Larger cookies can be made if desired.

Bake in a 375° F (190° C) oven for 10 - 20 minutes, until browned on the bottom.

Makes 2 dozen large cookies.

Lemon Meringue Squares

These easy-to-make squares are scrumptious.

CRUST

1/2 cup	Alpha Butter	125 mL
1/2 cup	sugar	125 mL
2	Country Morning egg yolks	2
1 tbsp	fresh Co-op Lemon Juice	15 mL
1 cup	Co-op Flour	250 mL
1/4 tsp	salt	1 mL
2 tsp	lemon rind	10 mL

MERINGUE

2	Country Morning egg whites	2
1/2 cup	sugar	125 mL
1/2 cup	chopped Co-op Almonds	125 mL

CRUST

Preheat oven to 350° F (180° C). In a medium bowl, cream together butter and sugar until light and fluffy. Beat in egg yolks and lemon juice. Stir in flour, salt and lemon rind. Evenly spread mixture into a greased 8 inch (2 L) square baking pan. Bake for 15 minutes, or until lightly browned. Remove from oven and cool. Increase oven temperature to 400° F (200° C).

MERINGUE

In a medium bowl, beat egg whites until stiff, moist peaks form. Gradually beat in sugar. Fold in almonds. Spread meringue evenly over cooled crust. Bake 5 - 7 minutes until meringue is lightly browned. Cool slightly and cut into 2 inch squares (5 cm).

Makes 16 squares.

Vanilla Pecan Bars

Sweet and gooey, these will be on the list of every pecan pie lover!

1	cup	Christie Vanilla Wafer, made into crumbs	250	mL
1/2	cup	Co-op Flour	125	mL
1/2	tsp	Magic Baking Powder	2	mL
1	cup	brown sugar	250	mL
1/2	cup	melted Alpha Butter	125	mL
2		Country Morning Eggs	2	
3/4	cup	brown sugar	175	mL
2	tsp	Co-op Vanilla	10	mL
1	cup	Co-op Chopped Pecans	250	mL

In a mixing bowl blend together wafer crumbs, flour, baking powder and brown sugar. Stir in melted butter until mixture is moist and crumbly. Press into a lightly greased 8 X 8 inch (2 L) square pan. Bake in a 350° F (180° C) oven for 10 minutes. Prepare filling.

In a mixing bowl beat eggs together. Add sugar and vanilla. Beat well. Stir in pecans. Pour evenly onto wafer crumb crust and return to 350° F (180° C) oven and continue baking for 20 - 25 minutes until topping is set. Cool completely. Cut into bars with a sharp knife.

Makes 20 - 24 bars.

See photo page 201

Edith's Crabapple Squares

A delicious combination of sweet and savoury in this shortbread type square.

3/4 cup	Alpha Butter	175 mL
1/4 cup	sugar	50 mL
1 1/2 cup	Co-op Flour	375 mL
Pinch	salt	Pinch
1 cup	shredded Armstrong Cheddar Cheese	250 mL
1/2 cup	finely chopped Co-op Pecans	125 mL
1 cup	crabapple jelly	250 mL

In a medium bowl cream together butter and sugar. Mix in flour and salt until combined. Add cheese and nuts. Mixture will be crumbly. Press 1/2 of this mixture into a greased 9 inch (2 L) baking pan. Spread with crabapple jelly. Sprinkle remaining crumb mixture over top.

Bake at 350° F (180° C) for 30 minutes or until golden brown. Cool well. Cut into squares.

See photo page 201

Cranberry Orange Drop Cookies

A delightful gift from the kitchen, anytime!

1 cup	Co-op Flour	250 mL
1 tsp	Magic Baking Powder	5 mL
1/2 tsp	Tone's Allspice	2 mL
1/2 cup	Alpha Butter	125 mL
1 cup	brown sugar	250 mL
1	Country Morning Egg	1
1 tsp	finely grated orange peel	5 mL
2 cups	Robin Hood Rolled Oats	500 mL
1 cup	Co-op Whole Cranberry Sauce	250 mL

GLAZE

1 cup	icing sugar	250 mL
1 tsp	grated orange peel	5 mL
2 tbsp	McCain's Orange Juice	25 mL
1 tsp	Co-op Vanilla	5 mL

In a mixing bowl stir together flour, baking powder and allspice. In another bowl cream together butter, brown sugar, egg and orange peel.

Add flour mixture, beat well. Stir in oatmeal and cranberry sauce.

On a lightly greased cookie sheet drop spoonfuls of batter. Bake in a 375° F (190° C) oven for 10 minutes until lightly browned.

Combine glaze ingredients and drizzle over warm cookies. Cool completely before storing.

Makes about 30 cookies.

See photo page 201

Fruity Shortbread

A traditional favourite simplified for easy baking.

1 cup	Alpha Butter	250 mL
3/4 cup	icing sugar	175 mL
1	Country Morning Egg	1
1 tsp	Co-op Vanilla	5 mL
2 cups	Co-op Flour	500 mL
1/2 cup	drained and chopped Co-op Maraschino Cherries	125 mL
1/2 cup	Co-op Mixed Peel	125 mL

In a large bowl with an electric mixer beat together butter and sugar until fluffy. Add egg and vanilla. Mix in flour. Stir in cherries and peel.

Form dough into 2 - 8 inch (20 cm) rolls about 1 1/2 inches (7 cm) in diameter. Wrap well and refrigerate at least 2 hours or until rolls are firm enough to slice.

Slice into 1/4 inch (1 cm) rounds and place on an ungreased cookie sheet. Bake in a 350° F (180° C) oven for 8 - 10 minutes until slightly golden around edges. Cool.

Makes about 60 cookies.

See photo page 201

Pink Lady Pie

A lovely light strawberry favourite! Be sure the marshmallows are fresh or the texture will be tough.

1 1/2 cups	Christie Graham Wafer Crumbs	375 mL
1/4 cup	softened Alpha Butter	50 mL
1/4 cup	sugar	50 mL
3/4 cup	McCain's Orange Juice	175 mL
3/4 lb	Co-op Marshmallows	375 g
1 1/2 cups	Alpha Whipping Cream (whipped)	375 mL
1	basket or more of fresh strawberries	1

Blend wafer crumbs with butter and sugar. Press into 9 inch (22 cm) pie pan. Bake at 375° F (190° C) for 5 minutes. Cool thoroughly.

Heat orange juice in double boiler. Add marshmallows and stir until melted. Cool mixture. Chill until partially set. Fold in whipped cream and berries. Pour in pie shell. Chill. Top with more whipped cream and those lovely "fresh strawberries" on top.

Makes 6 - 8 servings.

Fruity Pizza

An impressive and colourful dessert that is cut in wedges to serve.

1/2	pkg (900 g) oatmeal cookie mix	1/2
1/4 cup	water	50 mL
1	pkg (250 g) Co-op Cream Cheese, softened	1
1/2 cup	lemon spread	125 mL
1/2 tsp	grated lemon rind	2 mL
	Assorted fruit - kiwi, grapes, cherries,	
	strawberries, nectarines, peaches in season	

GLAZE

1/2 cup	Sunrype Apple Juice	125 mL
1 tsp	cornstarch	5 mL

Mix oatmeal cookie mix with 1/4 cup (50 mL) water in accordance with package directions. Press into pizza pan.

Bake at 375° F (190° C) for 10 minutes. Cool.

In a small bowl beat together cream cheese, lemon spread and lemon rind until smooth.

Spread evenly over cooled cookie crust.

Arrange sliced fruit as desired (see picture). Stir together apple juice and cornstarch - bring to boil either on top of stove or in microwave oven. Let cool.

Spoon over top of fruit for glaze.

Makes 8 - 10 servings.

Sweet Peach and Ricotta Dessert Pizzas

The rich, slightly tart taste of the ricotta cheese blends beautifully with the peaches.

1	pkg (450 g) Co-op Puff Pastry, thawed	1	
1 cup	ricotta cheese	250	mL
1/4 cup	sugar	50	mL
1 tsp	sherry	5	mL
1/2 cup	apricot jelly	125	mL
2	cans (14 oz/398 mL) Co-op Sliced Peaches, drained	2	

Preheat oven to 400° F (200° C). Cut pastry in half and roll out to a 12 X 12 inch (30 cm X 30 cm) square. Using a 5 inch (13 cm) wide bowl as a guide, cut out 6 circles of dough. (You may need to reroll dough scraps to get 6 circles). Repeat with remaining half of pastry. Turn up edges of each circle to form small rims. Place on an ungreased baking sheet. Set aside.

In a medium bowl, combine cheese, sugar and sherry. Spread mixture onto each pastry circle, dividing evenly. In a small saucepan, over low heat, melt jelly. Meanwhile, top each circle with 3 - 4 slices of peach. Spoon about 1 tsp (5 mL) of melted jelly over each circle. Bake for 20 minutes or until pastry is lightly browned and puffed. Serve warm or at room temperature.

Makes 12 pizzas.

Mocha Meringues

These look like individual cream tortes when put together.

MERINGUE

4	Country Morning egg whites	4
1 1/4 cups	icing sugar	300 mL
1 1/4 cup	Co-op Fine Unsweetened Coconut	300 mL

FILLING

3/4 cup	Alpha Whipping Cream	175 mL
1	pkg whipping cream stabilizer *	1
2 tbsp	cold, strong Co-op Coffee	25 mL
2 tsp	Brandy extract	10 mL
	Chocolate syrup	

* Whipping cream stabilizer is found in the pudding section.

Preheat oven to 275° F (140° C). Line 2 baking sheets with wax paper. With a pencil draw 12 circles 3 - 3 1/2 inches (8 - 9 cm). To make meringue, in a medium size bowl whip egg whites until stiff. Whip in half of sugar. Set aside. In another small bowl combine remaining sugar with coconut. Carefully fold into meringue mixture.

Spread meringue in the circle outlines, make 12 rounds. Bake in oven about 1 1/2 hours or until completely dry. Transfer to a wire rack while still warm.

To make filling beat whipping cream with stabilizer until stiff. Add coffee and brandy extract and beat another 20 seconds.

To assemble: Place 2 or more heaping tablespoons (30 mL) of whipping cream on 6 meringue rounds, using all of the whipped cream mixture. Sandwich the filling by topping it with another meringue round. To garnish, drizzle chocolate syrup and a dollop of whipped cream on top.

Makes 6 servings.

See photo page 10

Chocolate Caramel Oblivion

A scrumptious dessert with a soft caramel layer.

CRUST

1/3 cup	Alpha Butter melted	75	mL
1 1/3 cup	Christies Chocolate Crumbs	325	mL
1/4 cup	sugar	50	mL

CARAMEL LAYER

1	pkg (198 g) caramels (about 30 squares)	1	
2 tbsp	Alpha Butter	25	mL
1 tbsp	Alpha Whipping Cream	15	mL
2 tsp	Co-op Instant Coffee Granules (optional)	10	mL
1/2 cup	Co-op Chopped Pecans	125	mL

CHOCOLATE LAYER

1	pouch unflavoured gelatin	1	
1/4 cup	water	50	mL
1 1/2 cups	Alpha Whipping Cream	375	mL
1 cup	Co-op Chocolate Chips	250	mL

CRUST

In a medium bowl, combine crust ingredients. Press mixture into the bottom and sides of a deep 10 inch (25 cm) pie plate. Microwave on medium for 2 - 3 minutes or bake in a 350° F (180° C) oven for 10 minutes. Allow to cool.

CARAMEL LAYER

In a medium microwave safe bowl, place unwrapped caramels, butter, cream and coffee granules. Microwave on medium high for 2 minutes, or melt in a double boiler, or until caramels are melted. Stir after each minute to blend. Sprinkle pecans over crust. Pour caramel mixture on top.

CHOCOLATE LAYER

In a medium microwave safe bowl, dissolve gelatin in water. Let stand 1 minute. Add whipping cream and chocolate chips. Microwave on medium-high for 3 minutes, or until chocolate is melted and blended. Stir after every minute. Chill mixture for 30 minutes, or until mixture is consistency of raw egg white. Pour mixture over prepared crust. Refrigerate for 3 - 4 hours. Garnish with whipped cream. Let dessert sit at room temperature for 10 minutes before serving.

Makes 8 - 10 servings.

Decadent Ice Cream Sandwiches

Just like an "Eskimo Pie"!

1/2 cup	Alpha Butter	125 mL
1/3 cup	Co-op Cocoa	75 mL
2	Country Morning Eggs, lightly beaten	2
1 cup	sugar	250 mL
1/2 tsp	Co-op Vanilla	2 mL
1/2 tsp	salt	2 mL
3/4 cup	Co-op Flour	175 mL
1/2 cup	Co-op Chopped Pecans	125 mL
1 quart	Beatrice Ice Cream, slightly softened	1 L

Preheat oven to 350° F (180° C). Line a 10 X 15 inch (25 X 40 cm) cookie sheet with foil. Grease foil. In a medium size saucepan, melt butter, and add cocoa. Stir together and remove from heat. Add eggs, sugar, vanilla, and salt. Mix well. Stir in flour and nuts. Scrape mixture onto cookie sheet. Spread mixture evenly to cover. The mixture will be very thin, but the product will rise in baking. Bake 10 - 12 minutes or until brownie mixture is no longer shiny. Cool brownies for 1 hour.

Invert brownies and peel off foil. Cut in half. Spread ice cream on one half of brownies and place the other brownie half on top. Cover and place in freezer for 1 hour. Cut in 2 X 4 inch (5 X 10 cm) bars and serve.

Makes 8 bars.

Chocoholic's Anonymous

This cake has a truffle-like texture. Beware; a small slice goes a long way!

4 oz	bittersweet chocolate	125 g
4 oz	semi-sweet chocolate	125 g
1/2 cup	unsalted Alpha Butter, softened	125 mL
1/4 tsp	Tone's Cinnamon	1 mL
3	Country Morning Eggs, at room temperature	3

Preheat oven to 425° F (220° C). Grease a 7 inch (18 cm) spring form pan and line bottom with greased wax paper. Wrap the outside of the pan with two layers of aluminum foil to prevent seepage. Place spring form pan in a 10 inch (25 cm) cake pan to use as a water bath.

In the top of a double boiler, break the chocolates into pieces and add cinnamon and butter. Heat until fully melted, stir occasionally.

In a large size bowl, beat eggs for five minutes or until soft peaks form. Using a rubber spatula, fold in chocolate mixture. Mix together until no streaks remain. Pour mixture into prepared spring form pan. Set spring form pan into larger cake pan and surround it with 1 inch (2.5 cm) of very hot water. Bake for 5 minutes. Cover loosely with foil and bake an additional 10 minutes. Remove cake from oven and cool on a rack for 1 hour. Cover with plastic wrap and refrigerate for three hours. Remove from refrigerator 1/2 hour before serving time.

Makes 8 - 10 servings.

Chocolate Strawberry Torte

This deliciously rich chocolate sponge-cake combined with a creamy cheese filling tantalizes the taste buds.

CAKE BASE

2 tbsp	Alpha Butter	25	mL
1	square (1 oz/28 g) semi sweet chocolate	1	
1/2 tsp	Co-op Vanilla	2	mL
2	Country Morning Eggs	2	
1/4 cup	sugar	50	mL
1/4 cup	Co-op Flour	50	mL
1/4 cup	Co-op Cocoa	50	mL

FILLING

1	envelope unflavoured gelatin	1	
1/4 cup	water	50	mL
1	pkg (250 g) Co-op Cream Cheese	1	
1/2 cup	icing sugar	125	mL
1 cup	Alpha Whipping Cream	250	mL
2 cups	sliced strawberries	500	mL
	Strawberries to garnish		

CAKE

In a small bowl combine butter and chocolate. Melt together in microwave on medium or over a saucepan of simmering water, until smooth. Cool to room temperature.

In a large bowl beat together eggs, sugar and vanilla until triple in volume. This mixture should be thick and very pale.

Sift together flour and cocoa. Fold into egg mixture. Combine folding and drizzle in cooled chocolate and butter mixture until combined.

Pour into a greased 9 inch (23 cm) spring form pan and bake at 375° F (190° C) for 10 minutes. Cool.

FILLING

In a small saucepan or microwavable bowl sprinkle gelatin over cool water. Let stand 1 minute. Heat to boiling and stir until gelatin is dissolved. Set aside.

In a food processor or mixer beat cream cheese and icing sugar until soft. Continue beating and slowly drizzle gelatin into cream cheese.

In a medium bowl whip cream to soft peaks. Fold cream cheese into whipped cream. Fold in sliced strawberries.

Pour mixture evenly over cake base. Decorate with additional strawberries. Refrigerate 2 hours to overnight.

Makes 12 servings.

See photo page186

Chocolate Brownie Bombe

A 'bombe' is a layered rounded concoction of cake and ice cream.

BROWNIE BASE

3/4 cup	Co-op Flour	175 mL
1/3 cup	Co-op Cocoa	75 mL
1/4 tsp	salt	1 mL
1 cup	sugar	250 mL
1/2 cup	West Canola Oil	125 mL
2	Country Morning Eggs, lightly beaten	2
2 tbsp	Alpha Milk-2%	25 mL
1 tsp	Co-op Vanilla	5 mL
1/2 cup	Co-op Chopped Nuts	125 mL
1/2 cup	white chocolate chips	125 mL

In a medium mixing bowl sift together flour, cocoa, salt and sugar. Stir in oil, eggs, milk and vanilla until mixed. Add chopped nuts and white chocolate chips. Stir together. Grease and line an 8 inch (2 L) round pan. Pour brownie batter into pan. Bake at 325° F (160° C) for 30 - 35 minutes until toothpick inserted in centre comes out clean. Cool 5 minutes in pan. Turn out onto cooling rack, remove wax paper from bottom and cool completely.

2 litres	Beatrice Chocolate Ice Cream	2
1 litre	Beatrice Strawberry Ice Cream	1
2 cups	Beatrice Vanilla Ice Cream	500 mL
2 cups	Alpha Whipping Cream	500 mL
1/4 cup	icing sugar	50 mL
1/2 cup	broken peanut brittle	125 mL
	Chocolate shot	

Line a bowl 8 inch (20 cm) in diameter with plastic wrap.

Spoon softened chocolate ice cream into bowl covering the entire inside of the bowl to about 1 inch (2.5 cm) depth. If too soft return to freezer for 1/2 - 1 hour. Follow the same procedure with the strawberry then the ice cream. Place cooked brownie on top of softened ice cream. Return to freezer until hard.

Beat whipping cream and icing sugar until stiff peaks form.

Turn out of bombe bowl onto serving plate. Remove plastic wrap.

Ice bombe with whipped cream. Garnish with peanut brittle and chocolate shot.

Return to freezer. Remove from freezer 5 minutes prior to cutting. Cut with a large knife dipped in hot water.

Cherry Blossom Brownies

These squares taste like Black Forest Cake!

1	pkg Co-op Fudge Brownie Mix	1
1	can (19 oz/548 mL) E.D. Smith Cherry Pie Filling	1
1/4 cup	Co-op Chocolate Chips	50 mL
1/2 cup	Co-op Cream Cheese	125 mL
1/4 cup	sugar	50 mL
2	Country Morning Eggs	2
1 tsp	Co-op Vanilla	5 mL
2 tbsp	Co-op Flour	25 mL

Make brownie mix in accordance with package instructions for "cake brownie".

In a small bowl combine cream cheese, sugar, eggs, vanilla and flour.

Pour half brownie batter in bottom of a greased 9 X 13 inch (3 L) pan. Spread cherry pie filling over batter. Sprinkle chocolate chips evenly over pie filling. Drizzle with cream cheese mixture. Carefully spoon remainder of brownie batter over cream cheese mixture.

With a knife, make a few circles to marbleize the batter. Bake at 350° F (180° C) for 50 minutes. Cool. Cut into squares.

Makes 20 squares.

Scottish Toffee Tarts

*A spot of tea, comfortable chair and a wee sweet tart make
unwrapping the toffee all worthwhile.*

1 cup	Alpha Butter	250 mL
1/4 cup	icing sugar	50 mL
2 cups	Co-op Flour	500 mL
3	pkg (100 g) toffee	3
1/4 cup	Co-op Evaporated Milk	50 mL

In a mixing bowl combine butter, sugar and flour. Beat until a soft dough forms. Press spoonfuls of dough into small tart forms (24). Bake at 400° F (200° C) for 10 minutes until lightly golden.

In the top of a double boiler combine toffee and evaporated milk. Melt together until smooth. Spoon or pour into tart shells. Cool and store in air tight container in single layer.

Makes 2 dozen.

Fruit Braid

Soft summer tree fruits such as peaches, apricots, plums or pears team up deliciously with sweet almond paste and a golden puff pastry. (Almond paste is available in the bakery section).

1		pkg (454 g) frozen puff pastry, thawed	1	
1		pkg almond paste at room temperature	1	
3	cups	peeled and sliced soft fruit	750	mL
1/2	cup	Co-op Blanched Sliced Almonds	125	mL
1	tbsp	sugar	15	mL

Thaw frozen pastry. Roll out into a 12 X 9 inch (30 X 20 cm) rectangle on a lightly floured pastry board or countertop. Loosen pastry from rolling surface and move to ungreased baking sheet before continuing. With a sharp knife cut sides of pastry 2 inches (4 cm) into the centre horizontally down the long side of the rectangle. Keep the almond paste at room temperature to make it easier to handle. On a floured surface roll out to the same size as the uncut centre of the pastry. Gently move and place on top of the pastry. On top of the almond paste layer the fruit slices attractively. Then gently weave or braid the pastry "strands" alternately across the fruit to create a criss-cross pattern folding "strand" ends under the sides for a cleaner "finish". When completed sprinkle with blanched almonds and then with sugar.

Bake in a 350° F (180° C) oven for 30 - 40 minutes until pastry is puffed and golden. Cool slightly before serving.

Makes 10 - 12 struedel like slices.

Marian's Strawberry Pie

This took last summers vote as the favourite dessert of the season.

1	9 inch (23 cm) baked Co-op Pie Crust	1
4 cups	strawberries, divided	1 L
1/2 cup	sugar	125 mL
4 tsp	cornstarch	20 mL
Pinch	salt	Pinch
1/4 cup	water	50 mL
2 tsp	Co-op Lemon Juice	10 mL
4 cups	cleaned and hulled strawberries	1 L

In a small saucepan crush 1 cup (250 mL) strawberries. Bring to boil. In a measuring cup combine cornstarch, salt and water. Stir till cornstarch is dissolved. Add to strawberries. Stir and continue cooking until glaze is thick and transparent. Cool slightly, add lemon juice. Cool.

Place 3 cups (750 mL) strawberries point side up in the bottom of your pie crust. Pour glaze over strawberries and chill.

Makes 6 servings.

Strawberry Cheese Pie

A delightful mock cheesecake that can be prepared in minutes.

3 cups	sliced strawberries	750 mL
2 tbsp	sugar	25 mL
1	pkg (250 g) Co-op Cream Cheese	1
1	container (1-L) Co-op Frozen Whipped Topping	1
1	9 inch prepared graham wafer crust	1

In a small bowl combine strawberries and sugar, let stand 10 minutes.

In a food processor or with electric beater beat together cream cheese and strawberry mixture. Fold in whipped topping. Pour or spoon into graham crust. Garnish with fresh strawberries.

Refrigerate until serving.

Makes 6 servings.

Key Lime Chiffon Pie

With the coconut pie shell and rich lime flavour you'll swear you feel tropical breezes when you serve this treat!

COCONUT SHELL

2 cups	Co-op Shredded Coconut, toasted	500	mL
1/4 cup	brown sugar	50	mL
1/2 cup	Alpha Butter, melted	125	mL

Mix in a bowl. Firmly press into a 9 inch (23 cm) greased pie plate. Chill to firm.

LIME FILLING
SYRUP

1 cup	water	250	mL
1/2 cup	sugar	125	mL
1/4 cup	finely cut strips lime peel	50	mL

LIME CREAM

1/3 cup	lime syrup	75	mL
1	envelope unflavoured gelatin	1	
1/3 cup	fresh lime juice	75	mL
1/2 cup	sugar, divided	125	mL
2	Country Morning Eggs, separated	2	
4-5	drops, green food colouring (optional)	4-5	
1 cup	Alpha Whipping Cream	250	mL
1 tsp	Co-op Vanilla	5	mL

TO MAKE SYRUP

In a saucepan combine water and sugar. Heat to simmer. Stir in lime zest and simmer for 30 minutes. Strain, reserving syrup and lime zest.

FOR FILLING

Heat 1/3 cup of syrup in saucepan. Remove pan from heat and sprinkle with gelatin, let soften 1 minute. Then stir in lime juice 1/4 cup (50 mL) sugar, 2 yolks, and food colouring, if desired. Place over low heat, stirring constantly until mixture is thick and frothy, about 5 minutes.

Remove from heat and cool to room temperature.

Beat egg whites and 2 tbsp (25 mL) of the remaining sugar until stiff peaks form. Fold lime cream mixture into egg whites.

Beat whipping cream with remaining 2 tbsp (25 mL) sugar and vanilla until thick. Fold into egg lime mixture. Pour into pie shell. Garnish with reserved candied lime zest.

Chill several hours before serving.

Makes 6 - 8 servings.

Pumpkin Roll

The lemon and ginger compliments the pumpkin.

JELLY ROLL

6	Country Morning Eggs, room temperature	6
1 cup	sugar	250 mL
1 tsp	Co-op Vanilla	5 mL
Pinch	salt	Pinch
1 tbsp	Co-op Molasses	15 mL
1 cup	sifted cake flour	250 mL
1/4 tsp	Tone's Ginger	1 mL
1/4 tsp	Tone's Cinnamon	1 mL
Pinch	Tone's Ground Cloves	Pinch
1/4 cup	icing sugar	50 mL

FILLING

1 cup	Co-op Pure Pumpkin	250 mL
1/3 cup	icing sugar	75 mL
1 tbsp	grated fresh ginger	15 mL
2 tsp	grated lemon peel	10 mL
2 tsp	fresh Co-op Lemon Juice	10 mL
1 cup	Alpha Whipping Cream	250 mL

TO PREPARE PUMPKIN JELLY ROLL

Leave eggs on counter until room temperature to ensure that you get sufficient volume. Preheat oven to 350° F (180° C) placing rack to top 1/3 oven. Line a 10 X 15 inch (40 X 25 cm) jelly roll pan with wax paper.

In a large bowl beat together eggs, sugar, vanilla and salt until triple in volume. Add molasses.

Sift together flour and spices, fold into egg mixture. Pour onto prepared pan. Drop pan onto counter to release air bubbles. Bake 20 minutes until golden. Remove from oven. Run knife around sides of cake and let cake cool in pan.

Place a clean, dry tea towel on counter. Cover with waxed paper, cut slightly larger than cake on top. Sift icing sugar onto waxed paper. Turn completely cooled rack onto waxed paper and carefully roll with tea towel from long end. Set aside and prepare filling.

TO PREPARE FILLING:

In a small bowl, mix together pumpkin, sugar, ginger, lemon peel and lemon juice. Set aside. In a medium bowl, whip cream until stiff. Fold in pumpkin mixture.

Unroll cake. spread evenly with filling. Roll cake jelly roll style. Rewrap cake in wax paper and tea towel and refrigerate for 30 minutes to overnight.

Unwrap and place on serving dish seam side down.

Sprinkle with icing sugar if necessary.

Serve.

Makes 8 - 10 servings.

Easy Cassata

This quick variation of the traditional Italian dessert can be made a day ahead and kept in the fridge. Pick up the ingredients on your way home and put together in about 10 minutes.

1	cup	ricotta cheese	250	mL
2	tbsp	sugar	25	mL
1/2	tsp	Co-op Vanilla	2	mL
1		frozen pound cake	250	mL
3		semi-sweet chocolate squares	3	
1	cup	E.D. Smith Triple Fruit Rasberry, divided	250	mL
2	tbsp	unsalted Alpha Butter	25	mL
2	tbsp	brandy	25	mL

In a small bowl mix together ricotta cheese, sugar and vanilla. Set aside.

Cut cake horizontally into 4 even slices.

Set bottom slice on serving tray and spread with (1/4 cup (50 mL) cherry jam and 1/3 of ricotta cheese mixture. Repeat twice and end by placing top slice of cake on last.

In a small heavy bottomed saucepan melt chocolate. Stir in remaining cherry preserve and butter. Stir until melted. Add brandy.

Carefully spoon chocolate sauce on top of cake. Garnish with whipped cream. Slice and serve.

Makes 8 servings.

Tiramisu

Best if made a day in advance, this Italian style "trifle" is a fantasy of flavour and texture. The Winnipeg cream cheese is available in the Deli.

5	Country Morning Eggs, separated	5
1/2 cup	sugar	125 mL
2 cups	Winnipeg cream cheese	500 mL
1	pkg (200 g) lady finger biscuits	1
1/2 cup	strong Co-op Coffee	125 mL
1/4 cup	coffee liqueur	50 mL
1/4 cup	orange liqueur	50 mL
2	squares semi-sweet chocolate, grated	2

In a mixing bowl beat egg whites until foamy. Gradually add sugar while continuing to beat until stiff glossy peaks are formed.

In a separate bowl beat together egg yolks and cream cheese until smooth. Stir one-quarter of the yolk-cheese mixture into the egg whites. Then fold this egg white mixture back into the cheese mixture until just combined.

Prepare dessert in a large bowl (glass shows off the layers). Break biscuits into thirds and line bottom of bowl with one-quarter of the biscuits.

In a measuring cup stir together coffee and liqueurs. Drizzle one-third over dry biscuits. Spread with one-third of the cream-egg mixture. Sprinkle with one-third of the grated chocolate. Repeat layers two more times, ending with a topping of grated chocolate.

Keep refrigerated.

Makes 10 - 12 servings.

Cranberry Pecan Tart

A great dessert for special dinners such as Thanksgiving and Christmas.

TART SHELL

1 cup	Co-op Flour	250 mL
1/3 cup	sugar	75 mL
1/4 tsp	salt	1 mL
1/3 cup	Alpha Butter	75 mL
1	Country Morning Egg	1
2 tsp	water	10 mL

TART FILLING

1/4 cup	sugar	50 mL
1/2 cup	corn syrup	125 mL
2	Country Morning Eggs, lightly beaten	2
1/4 cup	McCain's Orange Juice	50 mL
1/2 tsp	grated orange rind	2 mL
1 cup	Co-op Whole Pecans	250 mL
1 cup	fresh or frozen cranberries	250 mL

TART SHELL

In a medium sized bowl, combine flour, sugar and salt. With a pastry cutter, cut in butter until the mixture is the texture of bread crumbs. Add egg and water and mix with a fork. To form dough, knead mixture until if forms a ball. Wrap dough in plastic wrap and refrigerate for 30 minutes. Heat oven to 375° F (190° C). On a floured surface roll out dough and place in greased 9 inch (23 cm) fluted tart pan. Prick tart shell with fork. Bake 10 minutes. Remove from oven and pat pastry down (it tends to get a puffy centre). Bake an additional 5 minutes.

TART FILLING

In a medium sized bowl, combine sugar, corn syrup, eggs, orange juice and rind. Place pecans and cranberries in bottom of tart shell. Pour tart filling over top. Bake 25 - 30 minutes or until crust is golden. Cool and serve warm or refrigerated.

Makes 8 servings.

Grapefruit Mint Sorbet

Refreshing and lively, this "ice" makes a light finish to any meal.

1/2 cup	sugar	125 mL
1 1/4 cups	water	300 mL
2 cups	Co-op Grapefruit Juice	500 mL
2 tbsp	chopped fresh mint	25 mL
2	egg whites	2

In a saucepan combine sugar and water, heat without boiling until sugar is dissolved. Then bring to a boil and simmer for 10 minutes, uncovered without stirring. Cool.

Add juice and mint. Pour into a bread pan, cover with foil and freeze until partially set.

In a food processor blend together egg whites and partially set sorbet. Return to pan and freeze at least 12 hours.

Allow pan to sit at room temperature for 10 minutes to soften before serving.

Makes 6 servings.

Rocky Road Cake

This is an easy one bowl cake.

1 cup	Robin Hood Quick Cooking Oats	250 mL
1/2 cup	West's Margarine	125 mL
1 3/4 cups	boiling water	425 mL
1 cup	brown sugar	250 mL
3/4 cup	white sugar	175 mL
2	Country Morning Eggs, beaten	2
1 1/2 cups	Co-op Flour	375 mL
1 tsp	Co-op Baking Soda	5 mL
1 tbsp	Co-op Cocoa	15 mL
1/2 tsp	salt	2 mL
1 cup	Co-op Chocolate Chips (divided)	250 mL
1/2 cup	Co-op Pecans	125 mL
1 cup	Co-op Miniature Marshmallows	250 mL

In a large mixing bowl combine oats and margarine. Pour boiling water over top of oats and let stand 10 minutes. Stir in sugars and eggs. Add flour, soda, cocoa, salt, 1/2 cup (125 mL) chocolate chips, pecans and marshmallows.

Stir until well combined. Pour into a greased 9 X 13 inch (3 L) pan. Sprinkle remaining chocolate chips on top. (Marshmallows will rise to the top and melt during cooking to form a sweet topping with the chocolate chips).

Bake in a 350° F (180° C) oven for 40 minutes.

Makes 16 squares.

The Ultimate Brownie

This recipe is a winner. It is surely from chocolate heaven.

1/2 cup	Alpha Butter	125 mL
3	squares, unsweetened chocolate, coarsely chopped	3
2	Country Morning Eggs	2
Pinch	salt	Pinch
1 cup	sugar	250 mL
1/2 cup	Co-op Flour	125 mL
2 tsp	Co-op Vanilla	10 mL
1	(85 g) white chocolate bar chopped into 1/2 inch (1 cm) pieces	1
1	(85 g) milk chocolate bar chopped into 1/2 inch (1 cm) pieces	1
1	(85 g) bittersweet chocolate bar chopped into 1/2 inch (1 cm) pieces	1

Line an 8 inch square (2 L) pan with foil, grease lightly. In a small saucepan melt butter over low heat. Remove from heat, stir in unsweetened chocolate. Set aside. In a large bowl beat eggs on high speed until foamy, about 30 seconds. Blend sugar with eggs. Beat 2 - 3 minutes until mixture is pale yellow and very thick. Pour butter chocolate mixture and vanilla into eggs. Continue beating until well blended. Stir flour into this mixture. Stir in broken chocolate bars. Pour into prepared pan. Bake 30 - 35 minutes at 325° F (160° C).

When cool, cut into squares.

Makes 16 brownies.

Pavlova Pie

This meringue based crust can be filled with any seasonal fruit, or mixture of fruits.

2	egg whites	2
1 1/2 cups	sugar	375 mL
1/2 tsp	Co-op Vanilla	2 mL
1 tsp	cornstarch	5 mL
1/4 cup	boiling water	50 mL

Place all ingredients in a large mixing bowl. Beat on high until smooth and stiff (about 12 minutes). Lightly grease a 9 inch deep pie plate. Dust with cornstarch shaking off excess. Spoon mixture into pie plate. Bake at 350° F (180° C) for 10 minutes. Reduce heat to 300° F (150° C) and continue baking for 45 minutes.

FILLING

1 cup	Alpha Whipping Cream	250 mL
1 tbsp	icing sugar	15 mL
2 cups	strawberries	500 mL

In a medium bowl, whip together cream and sugar, until stiff peaks form. Spoon on top of Pavlova and garnish with strawberries.

Makes 8 servings.

Warm Strawberry Orange Dessert

An easy barbecue dessert fit for your company.

4 cups	sliced strawberries	1 L
1 tsp	orange zest	5 mL
1/4 cup	McCain's Orange Juice	50 mL
1 tbsp	orange flavoured liqueur	15 mL
	OR	
1/4 tsp	Co-op Almond Extract	1 mL
1	(10 oz/284 mL) frozen pound cake	1
	Beatrice Vanilla Ice Cream	

In a foil baking dish place sliced strawberries. Combine orange zest, orange juice and liqueur in measuring cup. Pour over top.

Place baking dish on barbecue, stirring occasionally until the mixture comes to a boil.

In the meantime, slice pound cake into 1/2 - 3/4 inch (1 - 2 cm) slices. Place on grill and toast on both sides until golden.

Place a piece of cake and scoop of ice cream on a plate. Spoon hot strawberries and sauce over top. Serve.

Makes 8 servings.

Caramallows

Chewy and sweet. A welcome addition to homemade candy boxes.

1/4	cup	ground Co-op Walnuts	50	mL
1/4	cup	Co-op Shredded Coconut	50	mL
1		pkg (500 g) large marshmallows (about 30)	1	
30		toothpicks	30	
1/2	lb	caramels (about 40)	500	g
2	tbsp	water	25	mL

Mix walnuts and coconut together in a shallow dish, set aside. Insert toothpicks into the tops of marshmallows. Place caramels and water in a small microwave safe bowl. Microwave on medium high for 1 1/2 - 2 minutes. Stir, or melt over a double boiler, stirring constantly until smooth. Dip marshmallows in melted caramels and roll in nut mixture about half way up the marshmallow. Set on wax paper. Caramallows can be kept in a covered container.

Makes 30 caramallows.

Chocolate Marble Bark

Making chocolates is easier than you think!

1 cup	Co-op Blanched Almonds	250 mL
12 oz	semi-sweet chocolate	375 g
12 oz	white chocolate	375 g

Roast almonds by placing them on a cookie sheet and place under broiler for 1 - 2 minutes, or until browned. Take cookie sheet out and stir almonds, broil for an additional minute.

Break semi-sweet chocolate into small pieces and place in a microwave safe bowl. Microwave on medium high for 2 1/2 minutes or until chocolate has melted. Add half of the almonds to mixture and set aside. Follow the same procedure for the white chocolate, adding the rest of the almonds. On a cookie sheet covered with wax paper, pour chocolate in strips. Start with pouring one strip of dark chocolate and alternate with another strip of white chocolate. Continue until you have run out of chocolate. To get the marbled look, run a wooden spoon back and forth between the two chocolates, being careful not to overmix. Refrigerate bark until firm and break into pieces. Store refrigerated in a covered container.

Almond Brittle

Our microwave method helps take the guesswork out of candy making.

3/4 cup	sugar	175 mL
1/4 cup	brown sugar	50 mL
1/2 cup	corn syrup	125 mL
1 cup	Co-op Almonds, roasted	250 mL
1 tsp	Alpha Butter	5 mL
1 tsp	Co-op Almond Extract	5 mL
1/4 tsp	salt	1 mL
1 tsp	Co-op Baking Soda	5 mL

In a large microwave safe bowl combine sugar, brown sugar and corn syrup. Microwave at High for 5 minutes, making sure to stir the mixture every minute. Stir in almonds and microwave on High for 3 minutes. Stir butter, almond extract and salt into the hot bubbling mixture. Add the baking soda and stir until light and foamy. Pour mixture onto a greased cookie sheet. Let mixture cool for 1 hour and then break into pieces.

Store in a covered container.

Chocolate Dip

Use for dried fruit, nuts or strawberries.

1 cup	Co-op Semi-Sweet Chocolate Chips	250 mL
1/4 cup	shortening	50 mL

Place chocolate chips and shortening in a 2 cup (500 mL) microwave safe measure. Microwave on medium high for 1 minute. Stir. Microwave for 30 more seconds or until chocolate chips have fully melted.

If mixture hardens, it can be reheated.

Dip fruit and nuts in mixture. Set on waxed paper until hardened.

Makes enough for 30 pieces of fruit.

Chocolate Dipped Apricots

An easy, fanciful addition to a sweet tray.

| 1 | package (250 g) Co-op Dried Apricots | 1 |
| 1 | recipe chocolate dip (pg 199) | 1 |

Dip apricots into chocolate dip. Let excess chocolate drip off. Place on wax paper and let chocolate harden. Store refrigerated in a closed container.

Makes about 30 apricots.

Decadant Dates

A great gift for teachers, the postal carrier and other friends.

1	package (227 g) pitted Co-op Dates	1
6 oz	orange cream cheese	150 g
1	recipe chocolate dip (pg 199)	1

Cut cream cheese into 1/2 X 3/4 inch (1 cm X 2 cm) strips (orange cream cheese is found in the Co-op Deli). Cut open dates and insert cream cheese strips. Dip stuffed dates into chocolate dip and place on wax paper until chocolate hardens. Stuffed dates may be stored in the refrigerator in a closed container.

Makes about 40 dates.

with Thanks

We gratefully acknowledge the assistance of the following suppliers in making the production of this book possible:

Alpha Milk and Cream

Alpha Butter

Armstrong Cheese

Beatrice Foods

Best Foods Inc.

Bisquick - General Mills

Catelli Pasta

Christie Brown & Co.

E.D. Smith

Fleishmann's Yeast

Knorr Soup

Magic Baking Powder - Nabisco

McCain Foods Ltd.

Robin Hood

Sun-Rype

Tone's Spices

West Oil and Margarine

Yoplait Yogourt

My Favourite Recipes

My Favourite Recipes

INDEX

INDEX

INDEX

INDEX

INDEX